Make Your Woodworking Pay for Itself, Revised Edition

Make Your Woodworking Pay for Itself

JACK NEFF

BETTERWAY BOOKS
CINCINNATI, OHIO

Make Your Woodworking Pay for Itself, Revised Edition. Copyright © 1996 by Jack Neff. Printed and bound in the United States of America. All rights reserved. No part of this book may be reproduced in any form or by any electronic or mechanical means including information storage and retrieval systems without permission in writing from the publisher, except by a reviewer, who may quote brief passages in a review. Published by Betterway Books, an imprint of F&W Publications, Inc., 1507 Dana Avenue, Cincinnati, Ohio 45207. (800) 289-0963. First edition.

Other fine Betterway Books are available from your local bookstore or direct from the publisher.

00 99 98 97 96   5 4 3 2 1

Library of Congress Cataloging-in-Publication Data

Neff, Jack.
    Make your woodworking pay for itself / by Jack Neff.—
Rev. ed.
        p.   cm.
    Includes bibliographical references and index.
    ISBN 1-55870-418-3 (pbk. : alk. paper)
    1. Woodwork. 2. Home-based businesses. I. Title.
TT180.N36   1996
684′.08′0688—dc20   96-699
                                                     CIP

Editor: R. Adam Blake
Production editor: Bruce E. Stoker
Interior designer: Sandy Kent
Cover designer: Sandy Kent
Cover photo: Pamela Monfort Braun

Thanks to Mark Prince, owner of The Shaker Seed Box
    Company, 6656 Chestnut, Mariemont, Ohio 45227
    (513) 271-7100 for the generous use of props and space.

Betterway Books are available for sales promotions, premiums and fund-raising use. Special editions or book excerpts can also be created to specification. For details contact: Special Sales Manager, F&W Publications, 1507 Dana Avenue, Cincinnati, Ohio 45207.

DEDICATION

To Glenda and Matthew

ACKNOWLEDGMENTS

I'd like to thank the woodworkers, wood carvers, wood turners, and others whose knowledge and openness made this book possible and whose love of their craft, I hope, infuses it. In particular, thanks to Greg Adams, Ron Bower, Tom Clark, Gary Denzler, Tim Detweiler, Mary Anne Donovan, Joseph Ferola, Ed Gallenstein, Bob Hawkins, Glenn Huffman, Debbie Jones, Larry Joseph, Steven Martin, Jack McCarthy, Richard McKenzie, David Monhollen, Ray Murray, Rude Osolnik, Clark and Ronnie Pearson, Scott Phillips, Jamie Robertson, Norm Sartorius, David T. Smith, Rob Stigler, Michael Toombs and George Tyo. Special thanks to David Lewis, whose creativity and initiative launched this book. And my deep appreciation to the other minds and hands that helped shape this book, particularly editors Adam Blake, Bruce Stoker, Tom Howard and Kathleen Brauer.

ABOUT THE AUTHOR

Jack Neff is a freelance business writer living in Batavia, Ohio. He writes for newspapers and business and trade publications, and he is a regular contributor to *Woodshop News*.

Table of Contents

Introduction

You probably didn't take up woodworking to make money. You did it for the sheer love of it. The feel and beauty of a finely crafted piece of wood. The refreshing smell of a workshop. The absorbing joy of the work that makes hours go by so quickly. You turn to woodworking for these things and to get away from the daily grind of making money.

But money inevitably enters the picture. Woodworking gets more expensive all the time, as more and more power tools become "musts in any shop," and wood and supply costs rise. Even if you don't want to make a living as a woodworker, you may need some money just to finance or improve your hobby. If nothing else, a little income makes it much easier to justify all the expense to a skeptical spouse.

That's where this book comes in. Its aim is to help you make enough money to make your woodworking pay for itself. Maybe even a little extra. And, if you want, this book can even help you turn the hobby you love into a career you'll love even more.

Of course, you don't want to ruin a perfectly good hobby by doing it for money. Fortunately, you don't have to. You can have your cake, and make enough to buy the next one, too. This book is designed to show you ways to turn your woodworking projects into cash in the easiest ways possible. The extra money, in turn, can make your woodworking better and more enjoyable. Much of this book comes from the experiences of hobbyists and hobbyists-turned-pros who sold their work to create success beyond their wildest dreams. Everyone I talked with inresearching this book found selling their work added a new dimension to woodworking that made it more enjoyable, not less.

The first chapter can help make your woodworking more affordable even if you never sell a single Windsor chair or whirligig. It looks at ways hobbyists and pros alike have saved money on tools, wood and more—ways that virtually any small shop can duplicate.

The second chapter will take you on a tour through the many marketable facets of the woodworkers' craft, starting with smaller craft projects. Chapter three completes the tour, with a look at furniture making, wood carving and wood turning niches. There are literally thousands of items you can make and sell. These chapters let you see some of the areas up close to decide if they're right for you.

In chapter four, you'll find what kind of preparations you can make to show and sell your work. The chapter starts with a personal inventory you can take to help decide what kinds of selling options are best for you. Then it explores how to get ready to use those options.

Chapter five takes a closer look at the places to sell your work and the best ways to approach them. It includes some not-so-obvious tips on some of the more obvious ways to sell your work, such as craft fairs and craft stores. And it looks at some more unusual but potentially successful ways to sell your work.

Chapter six further unravels the mysteries of what selling your work will mean for you. It takes you step by step through the seemingly mysterious world of dealing with customers and setting fair prices. It also shows how to get through the paperwork and taxes as easily as possible.

Chapter seven looks at the logical decision any successful part-time woodworker must make: What do you do when your hobby starts turning into a business? It looks at some choices to consider before taking the plunge into a full-fledged business. It also considers alternatives for increasing your sideline income without giving up your day job or coming out of retirement.

How to handle the money you make from your woodworking is the subject of chapter eight. It includes tips on taxes, planning, contracts and cash flow. It's not necessarily fun, but it can make your life a whole lot easier.

Finally, chapter nine looks at how you can use your newfound source of woodworking income to make a more enjoyable hobby. That brings us back again to the point of this book, which is learning how to sell your projects to make your woodworking more enjoyable.

Shop Smarts— Saving Money and Space

Before you find ways to make money by selling woodworking projects, it makes sense to study your workshop. Consider what tools you really need, and create a plan for acquiring them. Find ways to squeeze every penny you can out of the dollars you spend on wood, tools and other supplies. The money you save by shopping smart and cutting waste adds substantially to the money you make. You don't have to pay tax on it, and it will make everything you sell more profitable. And, waste hurts the environment as much as your pocketbook.

Equipment Basics— What Do You Really Need?

Just which tools you need in your shop will depend on your projects. There are few tools that are absolutely essential if you are ingenious in finding a way around them. But there are some items most woodworkers would rather not do without.

Your Shop

How much room do you really need to set up shop? The answer always depends on what you do. A woodcarver may be able to work in the corner of a bedroom or basement. Some furniture makers may feel the need for a 1000-square-foot workshop, plus additional room for milling and storing wood.

Scott Phillips of the public television woodworking series *The American Woodshop* argues for relative simplicity. "You can look around my shop and see I'm not throwing a ton of money around here," says Phillips, whose show is taped mainly in the 800-square-foot garage/workshop outside his Piqua, Ohio, home. "I would guess in the total layout I've got about $14,000 worth of tools here. And I can build anything, from a beautiful wooden ship to a little toy top." To many beginning woodworkers, Phillip's workshop would be a dream shop, he concedes. But, he says, even $4000 in tools and a 12″×12″ space should provide most home woodworkers all the space and hardware they need, even if they're starting to sell their work.

Power Tools

Should you use power tools? This is a loaded question. Hand tool enthusiasts, some of whom are purists, see no reason why anyone would want to use power tools. And if the goal of your woodworking is strictly enjoyment, they're right. But to make a profit selling your work, or to get home projects done in a reasonable amount of time, most woodworkers have to use power tools.

Stationary Power Tools

- *Table saw.* For most woodworkers, either this or a radial arm saw is a must. The table saw is the first choice for the widest variety of woodworkers. Its adaptability and accuracy make it a shop favorite.
- *Radial arm saw.* This is a very adaptable tool, favored by many artisans. Although the table saw is the more popular choice among woodworkers, if you don't plan to do a lot of ripping stock or sizing sheets of plywood, the radial arm saw may be your best bet if you can only have one or the other.
- *Band saw.* Its versatility in making curved, irregular, beveled or straight cuts makes the band saw a staple in most shops. A jigsaw or portable saber

saw may be nice extras, and they're cheaper; but the band saw should get a higher priority.

- *Drill press.* You really have to have a portable drill with a drill guide, but a drill press is also nice to have. You can use either, but it takes a little more practice and skill to use a portable drill.

- *Lathe.* Though you can easily do without it for many projects, adding a lathe opens up many more project possibilities. Even if you don't turn decorative bowls, the lathe is a valuable tool for spindles, legs and even Christmas ornaments.

- *Jointer.* If you can afford it and have space, the jointer is the best tool for straightening edges, planing stock edges, beveling or chamfering stock, or cutting tapers and rabbeting stock edges.

- *Surfacer or planer.* Used to plane one face or edge of a board parallel to another face. One of the newer, less expensive and less bulky lightweight models will do the job fine if you buy wood that has been surfaced to within $\frac{1}{16}''$ by the mill. But you can get along without one of these if you buy dimensional stock or take rough material to a bigger shop and rent time on a big planer. The surfacer or planer is one of the last tools on the "to buy" list for most small shops.

Power Hand Tools

- *Portable drill.* A must-have. A handheld power drill can also be used as an electric screwdriver even if you don't need it as a drill.

- *Router.* This portable power tool is indispensable for shaping wood edges and cutting a variety of joints. Since freehand routing requires considerable skill and is impossible for small pieces that can't be clamped, you'll probably want a router

table, which provides for the router to be secured upside down and stock to be fed past it using adjustable fence guides.

- *Circular saw.* A useful tool if you need to cut rough stock to length, it can also be used as an inexpensive alternative to larger, more expensive tools, as we'll see later.

- *Sander.* Stationary sanders are too big and expensive to be practical for most woodworkers, some of whom believe power sanders of any kind should not be used on fine woodworking projects. This ultimately boils down to a question of personal philosophy and the type of work you do.

- *Spline or biscuit cutter.* A biscuit cutter is nice if you do a lot of biscuit joints. But a cheaper alternative is a $\frac{5}{32}''$ slot-cutting router bit that will let your router take on this job, too.

Non-Power Tools

Besides the big-ticket power items, every woodworker needs several other basic tools:

- Pencils, chalk and scratch awl
- Bench rule and tape measure
- A knife
- Miter and marking gages
- Planes and spokeshaves
- Layout squares and triangles
- Protractor
- Calipers
- Set of cabinetmaker's chisels and gouges
- Cabinet and glue scrapers
- Set of hand files
- Set of rasps
- Rubber mallet
- Claw and tack hammers
- Pliers

- Vise grips
- Numerous wood and metal speed clamps
- Spring clamps
- Bar or pipe clamps
- Sharpening tools

Tool Needs for Specialties

For carvers and turners, tool needs are far simpler and less expensive than for furniture makers. Here are some basic requirements for these groups.

Carvers

For whittlers, a knife. For chain saw carvers, a chain saw. These specialties are surely the least demanding of all woodworking areas in terms of equipment. Things are a little more complicated for other carvers. But not much.

- *Band saw.* This is the tool of choice for carvers in the preliminary shaping of blocks. You can use handsaws if you're a purist or want to keep expenses and dust to a minimum. But a band saw will make your life easier.
- *Gouges and chisels.* A basic set will suffice for a while at least. But finding just the right gouge or chisel for each job is a unique part of the craft. Cincinnati master wood-carver Jack Giglio has accumulated a set of 300 chisels, many of which he crafted himself and which he tracks by carving a distinctive handle for each. Even furniture makers will find a set of gouges and chisels useful for carving a touch of elegance into their work.
- *High-speed grinding tools.* (Dremel or Foredom, for example.) These are undeniably valuable for

final detail and hard-to-get-to places on carvings if nothing else. Whether they should be used for more is debatable. Drawknives, spokeshaves, rasps and multibladed forming tools can also be used to remove wood almost down to the final shape, though this will take longer. The big plus with non-power tools is less dust both on the floor and in your eyes and lungs. A wide variety of attachments are available to create different effects.

- *Grinding wheel.* A must to keep all those chisels sharp and to customize blades to individual tastes and jobs.

Bowl and Sculpture Turners

Bowl and sculpture turners have by far the simplest tool needs of all. Though many have gravitated into this specialty from a more general woodworking background and already have a shop full of power tools, this specialty really only requires:

- *A good wood lathe,* of which there are many to choose.
- *Turning chisels,* including a gouge for rough shaping of square stock and cutting coves, the skew to smooth rough turning, the round nose to smooth round stock and cut coves, the spear point for decorative cuts, and the parting tool to cut shoulders near beads and coves.
- *Grinding wheel* for sharpening lathe tools.
- *Band saw.* Many turners use a band saw to do rough shaping on blocks, remove burls from logs, etc.
- *Turners* can do without power sanders in many cases, because the lathe or a drill press with a sanding drum can handle most of it.

Of course, there has been a profusion of turning tools developed over the years for highly specialized tasks. One of the best sources for unique turning tools is *The Woodturners Catalog.*

Inexpensive Equipment Shortcuts

Sometimes, it seems like woodworkers and the toolmakers who serve them do more basic research and development than all of corporate America. Much of that research goes into more expensive tools with more bells and whistles. But sometimes there's a new product that saves money ingeniously.

- For under $150 you can turn a circular saw into a miter box and radial arm saw. A Canadian product called Trimtramp mounts a handheld circular saw on a parallel track with the blade guard above the stock being cut. You can pull the saw through the workpiece like a radial arm saw, allowing you to miter and crosscut boards up to 16″ wide. By adjusting the depth and angle of the blade, you also can make bevels, dadoes, rabbets and other joint cuts.

- A $40 kit from Sears lets a router do the work of a plate joiner for about $100 less than the cost of a dedicated plate joiner. The Sears Bis-Kit System is designed for Sears routers but with a few modifications works on any other routers with a base of 6″ or less. It won't cut biscuit slots in the middle of plywood or on the face of a board, but it will handle the usual edge plate-joining needs of most projects.

- California woodworker Andy Anderson developed a system that allows a router to do tapering and fluting of columns like a lathe. His Woodchuck Indexing Router System, sold by Phantom Engineering, allows some wood turning cuts to be made by manually rotating a piece of wood.

The Cooperative Solution

No matter how many ways you find to save money, the cost of establishing a home workshop can be prohibitive. For many people, the choices are going deeply into hock, buying low-priced equipment that may not provide adequate power and durability, or severely limiting the range of projects. But a logical choice that few people consider is sharing workshop space and tools with other woodworkers. If you can find enough friends or fellow woodworkers and the right space, consider starting your own co-op group. It could be a great way to start a sideline business or expand your woodworking hobby.

A sharing arrangement can work several ways. One is an outright cooperative, in which shop space is collectively managed and/or owned. In other cases, several woodworkers lease space in a building or factory. They share some equipment and space with each other or the owner. You may consider renting space and machine time from an established woodworking shop to get access to tools you need but don't have. Schools and clubs sometimes rent shop time, too, and you may be able to make use of their arrangement. To find shops that might be interested, check classified listings of woodworking publications or ask around at tool or lumber retailers.

It works somewhat like a long router table over a lathe. But the workpiece doesn't spin at high speeds. Instead, it can be gradually advanced a few degrees at a time on an indexing plate while a router shapes it. A kit to build the system costs $89 ($12 extra for all the hardware needed to build it). A home-shop version that handles columns up to 7″ in diameter costs $289. And a pro-shop version that handles columns up to 9″ and is constructed with welds rather than rivets costs $395.

While it's nice to save money, keep in mind that your time is also valuable. Trying to extend a tool to cover additional uses usually involves some time to convert the equipment. You might save some money, when you're strapped for cash, by making your equipment do double duty. But your long-term goal should be to make some additional money to purchase more tools and make your woodworking more efficient and enjoyable.

For up-to-date information about jigs and other shortcuts to make your woodworking life easier and less expensive, subscribe to woodworking publications. *Woodshop News* does a particularly good job of finding ideas for jigs and other innovations around the country, plus reviewing cost-effective new tools.

Do You Need a Computer?

The answer is "probably not." With so many other tools to buy, $2000 or so for a new computer system probably isn't at the top of your list. Nevertheless, a computer can be an invaluable resource for a woodworking hobbyist—particularly one who's venturing into business. And if you can meet other family needs with the computer at the same time, it's a great investment. Here are a few ways a computer can help:

- *Bookkeeping.* Relatively inexpensive and fairly easy-to-use software often can help you keep your books much more easily.
- *Databases.* You can keep an electronic file folder of retailers who buy, or might buy, your work, past customers, suppliers, craft shows, etc.
- *Mailing lists.* You can use those databases to generate mailing lists rapidly to keep in touch with past—and possibly future—customers.
- *Marketing materials.* Software for creating sim-

ple flyers and brochures gets simpler all the time. Though a graphic artist can do a much more presentable job, you can probably do the basics yourself.

- *On-line exchanges with other woodworkers.* The information available on the Internet and the World Wide Web grows constantly, and you can expect growing numbers of woodworking publications to develop on-line editions, too. If you do buy a computer system, spring for the extra $200 or so for a modem. It will be well worth your investment. Among the most popular of the on-line woodworking news groups is "rec.woodworking" available through the UseNet. This is a very popular group, with as many as 100 postings daily. Subjects span a wide range, including how to buy and use tools, project ideas, how to save money on buying wood, and where to find hard-to-find hardware. All of this is available for free, though you will have to pay an Internet access provider to get there.
- *CD-ROM information.* For now, CD-ROM woodworking titles are scant. But that's no reason not to outfit your computer with a CD-ROM, which is well worth the roughly $200 investment. Even if you only use a CD-ROM drive as an electronic phone directory, it's worth it. These directories, which retail for $50 to $100, give you access to every business and home phone number in the United States. They're great for locating potential suppliers or customers. And the savings in directory assistance charges alone could, in some cases, pay for the directory.

"Outsourcing" Parts

No matter how many tools you have, you may not be able to make everything you need for every project

Finding Resources on the Internet

One visit to the Internet's popular and rapidly growing World Wide Web sector gives you an idea of how it got its name. The Web is a series of links among sites, called home pages. If you drew a map of how these sites are linked together, it might look a lot like a spider's web, only not so well organized. Of course, drawing a map is impossible because web sites are constantly going up, coming down, and moving—much like the spiders' webs that are the system's inspiration.

Even so, there's plenty for woodworkers to gain from the Web. It's so popular because it offers enhanced graphics and tons of detailed information that would take you an impossibly long time to acquire any other way. What you can download for free from the Web, from pictures to catalogs to computer-aided drafting programs, grows daily.

Accessing the Web requires a computer system, a modem and an access provider. The big three providers—CompuServe, Prodigy and America OnLine—each offer Internet and Web acccess along with their own proprietary service features. Usually, these providers give you five hours a month for access to all services, with hourly charges for additional time. There is also built-in Web browser software that provides you easy-to-use access to the full graphic capabilities of the Web sites you visit. Some Internet access providers will charge higher monthly rates for unlimited access. If you plan to be "on-line" and using the Internet more than 10 hours a month, these providers deserve a look. These may not come with their own built in browsing software; but you can remedy this fairly quickly by visiting the "Netscape" home page (http://www.netscape.com) and downloading the free browsing software. At this time, Netscape software is still the best browsing software around, but others will surely be giving it a run for its money.

As of the end of 1995, there were already dozens of Web sites dedicated to woodworking. As this area of the Internet explodes, there will doubtless be hundreds or thousands within a few years. Trying to list them all, or even all the best ones, is impossible. Fortunately, thanks to the nature of the World Wide Web, you should be able to access the new ones from the old ones. Below are some of the top woodworking Web sites as of this book's most recent revision. Use these as starting points for exploring the Web on your own. The "URLs" listed are the site identifying names that you'll need to enter into your browser software to get to these sites.

- *W⁵: Wood Working on the World Wide Web* (http://www.iucf.indiana.edu/~brown/hyplan/wood.html). This is a forum for discussions with other woodworkers providing links to numerous other sites and several useful downloadable files, including an index to *Woodsmith* magazine and CAD packages.
- *Woodweb* (http://www.woodweb.com). This site provides access to manufacturers of wood products, articles from *Wood & Wood Products* and *Custom Woodworking business* magazines and more. You can access the *Woodworker's Guide to the Internet* through this site at (http://woodweb.com/mpguide.html).
- *The Woodworking Catalog* (http://www.woodworking.com). This offers a listing

of several furniture shops and suppliers, a featured oompany each month and such valuable downloadable tools as "Woodpro," a lumber database and wood selection system.

- *Jim Rochés Woodpage* (http//www.cs.rochester.edu/u/roche/wood.html). This includes a file of frequently asked questions (FAQs) from the popular rec.wood-working newsgroup, plus a wood toxicity table and more.
- *The Global Furniture Network* (http://www.gfurnet.com/gfn). This site has manufacturers' catalogs, industry newsletters, a reference guide to furniture terms and other good ways of staying abreast of the industry.
- *The Yahoo Guide* (http://www.yahoo.com). This is the chief of the World Wide Web directories. At no cost, you can search here for anything that appears in most of the Web universe, at least any page run by someone with enough moxie to take the simple steps needed to list it here.

in your own shop. Especially when you're just starting out and your shop isn't completely outfitted, you may need to turn to other woodworkers or vendors for help. Beginning furniture makers may not have the skills to do some of the detailed carving they would like to see in a piece. And for moldings, it's usually cheaper or nearly the same cost to buy what you need from a millwork shop than to make them yourself. Even full-time professional shops often sub-contract work. For instance, a small shop that specializes in dining room tables often contracts out production of chairs. Some shops outsource finishing to finish specialists.

The pros of buying some parts of your work ready-made from others include:

- Needing fewer machines around the shop.
- Possibly getting better work on a specialized item than you could do yourself.
- In some cases, reducing turnaround time on a project with a short deadline.
- Saving space in the shop by eliminating the need for some machines.

The cons of buying someone else's work include:

- Less assurance of quality. In some cases, you may be buying a pig in a poke.
- Less satisfaction in the finished product because you didn't make all of it. Also, some craft shows and stores require that all of your work be hand-crafted, except the hardware.
- Difficulty finding the right pieces for your project in terms of size, wood, etc.

You're probably better off building all the parts yourself if your project is relatively simple from the woodworking standpoint, such as birdhouses. The same is true if you make something highly specialized, such as art or fine custom furniture, for which it would be almost impossible to find appropriate prefabricated parts.

Here are some options for "outsourcing," should you decide to go that route.

- *Mail order.* Woodworking publications advertise vendors interested in selling off-the-shelf moldings and turnings.
- *Local woodworkers' supply stores.* They may have what you need or be willing to mill a piece to your specifications.

- *Other woodworkers.* This is probably the best option, because you can begin to forge partnerships that could improve everyone's work without sacrificing handcrafted quality. Woodworking clubs are one way to make such contacts. But if your club only has furniture makers, you may want to make inquiries of your own to local or national turners' and wood-carvers' groups. If you can get enough different woodworkers involved, it may be practical to set up a barter system in which everyone exchanges work based on points rather than dollars. That helps ease cash flow problems, but you've got to be assured that you'll actually need to draw out as many points as you put into the system. Otherwise, you're just giving your work away.

Sourcing Wood— Some Pointers

An artisan is almost always at a disadvantage in buying materials and supplies compared to a large company. Some of the cooperative efforts mentioned earlier could help. But you'll also need some savvy in sourcing your wood to help even the score. Here are some basic pointers that can help.

Softwoods and Hardwoods

Generally, softwoods are softer than hardwoods. But, the terms "softwood" and "hardwood" are somewhat misleading, since some hardwoods, like basswood, are actually softer than some softwoods, such as Douglas fir. The real distinction is that softwoods come from coniferous trees (evergreens with needles) and hardwoods come from deciduous trees (those with flat, wide leaves that fall off in autumn).

Most furniture and woodcrafts are made from hardwoods, which generally are more expensive. Cheaper softwoods are generally used in home construction. The resilience that makes softwoods good in a house frame is less appreciated on the exposed surface of a coffee table. But more expensive white and yellow pine may be used in country-style pine furniture and accessories.

Open and closed grains are another important distinction. All softwoods are close-grained, i.e., they have small pores or no pores. Hardwoods can be either open or close-grained. Open-grain hardwoods are porous, making them harder to finish—but they're also more likely to have the beautiful grain figures that add so much value to projects. Close-grained hardwoods are easier to finish but have less grain figure.

Hardwood grades are based on minimum board sizes and percent of usable stock. The larger the board and the greater the usable portion, the more valuable it is. Here's a rundown of the grades, which have been in effect since 1932 under rules of the National Hardwood Lumber Association.

- *Firsts and Seconds*—These are usually combined as the grade FAS, with the percentage of firsts in the mix required to be 20 to 40 percent, depending on the species of lumber. For both firsts and seconds, minimum board size is $6'' \times 8'$. Minimum percent of usable stock is $91\frac{2}{3}$ percent for firsts and $83\frac{1}{2}$ to $91\frac{2}{3}$ percent for seconds, depending on the total surface measure and number of cuttings. Firsts and seconds are very expensive, and unnecessary for many projects where both sides of the board don't show.
- *Selects*—Minimum dimensions: $4'' \times 6'$. Percent usable stock must be $83\frac{1}{3}$ to $91\frac{2}{3}$ percent on best face, based on the same criteria as seconds for one side of the board. The back side must meet

the criteria of the next lowest grade, No. 1 Common. For most purposes, selects are as good as seconds but at a lower price.

- *No. 1 Common*—Minimum dimensions of $3'' \times 4'$, with 66⅔ percent minimum usable stock for surface measure of 3 square feet or more. Woodworkers have varying opinions on when common grades should be used. Some feel this grade is not suitable for most fine woodworking projects, with the exception of some smaller projects or parts of projects. Others feel that common grades should be used for any short, narrow cuttings. You should consider whether the smaller widths and percentages of usable stock you get will meet your needs. The money you save on lumber may end up as waste on scrap or in labor making extra cuts.

- *No. 2 Common*—Same minimum size as No. 1, but minimum usable stock of 50 percent. Not usually available from retail lumber dealers, it can be found at bigger lumber or distribution yards, usually with a minimum purchase of 1000 board feet.

- *Sound Wormy*—Sounds funny. Actually, has same requirements as No. 1 Common or better except that wormholes, knots and other imperfections are allowed in the cuttings.

- *No. 3 Common*—Same minimum size as No. 1 Common, but only 33⅓ percent usable stock for No. 3A and 2 percent for No. 3B.

These are but a few of the many factors to take into account in selecting wood. Many of your decisions will be aesthetic and on a per-project basis. To make the best decisions, experience and the advice of fellow woodworkers is vital. Some lumber dealers may also be invaluable honest brokers who can steer you in the right directions.

The definitive source on wood is *The Encyclopedia of Wood*, written by the knowledgeable folks at the Forest Products Laboratory in Madison, Wisconsin. The laboratory can also help with individual inquiries, identifying woods and their special properties. For good general advice about wood and tools, the *Woodworker's Handbook* by Roger W. Cliffe is comprehensive and valuable.

Lumber Cost Factors— Maximizing Value

Several factors besides grade figure into the cost of lumber: how rare the species of wood, regional supply and demand, transportation costs, whether it's surfaced and more. But according to *Woodshop News* in November 1991, the factors shown in the sidebar "What You Pay for Lumber" made up the retail price of retail FAS lumber that was S2S (surfaced on two sides), R1E (ripped on one edge), and sold at no minimum quantity for $2.91 per board foot. (See page 10.)

This breakdown gives you some idea of where you can save money on lumber. If you could work with lumber directly from the sawmill and kiln-dry it yourself, you might save as much as half the cost of buying it at a retail lumber store. Buying lumber directly from a distribution yard and surfacing and ripping it yourself could (in theory) save you more than 40 percent. (Note that this percentage varies considerably, and may amount to as little as 5 percent.) Of course, the cost of the extra equipment also must be considered, plus the overhead of storing the wood and the quantities you would need to buy directly from the mill or distribution yard.

One way you might try to beat the high cost of wood is by milling your own—particularly if you live on wooded property or have the means of getting discarded trees from neighboring homes and farms. Charles Self's *Woodworker's Guide to Selecting and*

Milling Wood (1994, Betterway Books) is an excellent resource on how to do this. If you have the space and the money, a portable mill can eventually pay for itself. Or you might be able to pool your resources with your local woodworkers' club to buy a portable mill and cut your own wood.

While it's important to be frugal, keep in mind that, next to your craftsmanship, the wood you use is the most important ingredient for the success of any project. Skimping on the quality or amount of wood can in many cases more than pay for itself by setting your project apart from all the others and allowing you to charge a higher price.

Being a Frugal Woodworker

Here are a few other ways to cut the high cost of lumber.

- *Avoid exotics.* Not only are exotic hardwoods expensive, but they're increasingly frowned upon by the buying public which feels (rightly or wrongly) that using them contributes to the destruction of rain forests. There are plenty of beautiful native hardwoods to use. And for colorful inlays, you can buy exotic scraps from other woodworkers or shops that make larger projects with exotics, or buy alternative exotic woods, which are coming into the U.S. through sustainable forestry projects in Mexico, Peru and some other countries. Using them doesn't deplete the rain forests. But the working characteristics of these woods, which are relatively new to U.S. woodworkers, do take some time to learn.

- *Use high-quality plain-sawn oak instead of quartersawn.* Plain-sawn or flat-sawn lumber is cut so that the annual rings of the tree run from edge to edge. Quartersawn involves quartering the log first, then cutting toward the center of the tree to produce rings that are perpendicular to the face of the stock. Most logs are flat-sawn, because it produces a better lumber yield and has better figures than quartersawn in most cases. But with oak and a few other species, quartersawn logs produce beautiful flake figures and command a premium. Even flat sawing, however, produces a few boards with that same figure. Some mills and stores will sell these special flat-sawn boards at a premium, but some don't because they don't want to bother with sorting.

- *Use "found" wood.* This isn't practical for every woodworker or project, but for many, it's a godsend. Some woodworkers, particularly turners and carvers, work with found wood and little else. Rude Osolnik (see page 40) makes most of his internationally acclaimed turned bowls from burls he finds on his land in Berea, Kentucky, or in other forests. Turner Joseph Ferola (see page 89) leaves his card with people when he sees a tree in their yard that looks sick and offers to cut it down for them in exchange for the wood. Others who know of his work just call him when a tree falls. He usually rewards such kindness with a turned object for the benefactor. Birdhouse-maker Mary Anne Donovan (see pages 73-74) has drawn her materials from such diverse sources as leftovers from a rehabbed house and Salvation Army Thrift Stores, where she found wooden forks and production turned items that she incorporated into her work. Some salvage stores have parts of antique furniture, moldings and other fixtures from old homes and offices that can be perfect for reassembly. Or, you can get into salvage yourself by attending auctions or being on the lookout for older homes and buildings destined for the wrecking ball.

Retail and distribution yard prices are averages based on surveys of red oak lumber in the Northeast in July 1991, and are used for illustrative purposes only. Though costs have risen more than 20 percent since then, the chart still gives a good idea of how cost factors break down. The truckload price is for kiln-dried lumber, sold on a gross tally, and is an average. Prices will vary widely from region to region due to market conditions and other variables. Transportation cost of 8 cents/bf is based on an industry average of $50/mbf. But trucking lumber from the West Coast to the East could cost up to $150/mbf, tripling the transportation cost. Lumber processing costs also vary. Information on pricing was obtained from a *Woodshop News* telephone survey plus F. Thomas Milton, extension specialist in forest products at the University of Minnesota, and George Barrett, publisher of the *Weekly Hardwood Review*.

LARRY HAND ILLUSTRATION. REPRINTED WITH PERMISSION. WOODSHOP NEWS COPYRIGHT 1991.

What you pay for lumber

… and what your dollars buy at each level of the marketplace

Retail Lumber Store: $2.91/bf
(S2S, R1E, no minimum quantity)

Retail markup: 92¢/bf, including overhead, handling costs and profit margin

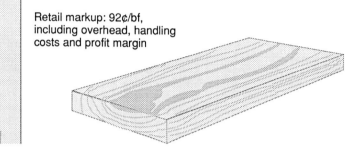

Ripping 1 edge: 15¢/bf

Surfacing 2 sides: 15¢/bf

Distribution Yard: $1,690/mbf
(rough-sawn lumber, 1,000-bf quantities)

Markup: 27¢/bf, including overhead, storage, handling costs and profit margin

Transportation: 8¢/bf

Shrinkage: 14¢/bf

Sawmill: $1,200/mbf
(rough-sawn lumber, truckload quantities)

Sawmill markup: 51¢/bf, including overhead, handling costs and profit margin (for FAS only; markup for lower grades is less)

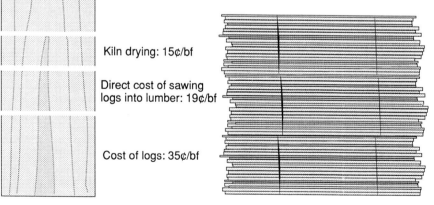

Kiln drying: 15¢/bf

Direct cost of sawing logs into lumber: 19¢/bf

Cost of logs: 35¢/bf

Don't Build or Buy More Than You Need

Having lots of material around can give you a sense of security, or inspiration to get to work. From a financial perspective, though, it's a burden. To lower your costs and your risk, it makes sense to have as little material, and as little inventory of finished work around as possible. Not only does that save precious shop space, but it also decreases the amount of money tied up in pieces that don't offer immediate monetary return.

Doing this, however, is a lot harder than saying it. Ideally, you would never build a piece until you had an order in hand for it. Then, you would quickly secure the materials and start to work. This is possible if you do strictly custom work, but if you have any production items or rely on unpredictable selling outlets, it's hard to do. If you rely on craft shows for much of your sales, for instance, needs for finished work can be unpredictable. Even if you have experience at that craft show, things change from year to year depending on weather, competing events in town and other unforeseen circumstances. Your woodworking life may be more predictable if you rely on shops to buy your work. But many shops want fast turnaround time for repeat orders, because their income depends on having stock without tying up too much cash in their inventory. To meet their needs, you may need some inventory of finished product, or at least enough materials on hand to get an order out.

Savings From the Scrap Heap

Shrinking landfill space around the country is driving up trash hauling costs while raising environmental consciousness. So, even if the cost of wood doesn't make you conserve, the cost (not only in dollars) of hauling it away should. Here's a list of ways you can salvage scrap.

- Heating with a wood stove and scraps is the chosen method of disposing of scraps for most woodworkers. But you have to be careful not to use particle board or glued wood products, because they tend to overheat and can release cancer-causing chemicals into the air.
- Organize projects to reduce scraps by using pre-planned cuts.
- Give or sell your scrap to carvers or turners who can use it. Even if you don't generate income, you may generate favors that can help you later.
- Organize your scrap by size and type of wood using shelf slots or cardboard tubes. Knowing where to find scrap makes it much likelier you'll use it when the need arises.
- Give your scrap away to schools that may be able to use it in shop classes.
- Donate scrap to farms and stables for animal bedding. But don't give them walnut or fruit woods or any chemically treated or manufactured woods, which can harm the animals.

Safety: Inexpensive Ways to Keep Your Shop Safe

Woodworkers suffer work-related injuries at roughly twice the national average, and at a rate higher than coal miners, according to the Bureau of Labor Statistics. And they have the Occupational Safety and Health Administration to look out for their well-being—at least in theory. Only common sense can prevent individual artisans from victimizing themselves relentlessly with unsafe working conditions. And many do. Making money with your woodworking shouldn't literally cost you an arm and a leg, or damage your health in any other way. With that in mind, here's a checklist of inexpensive ways to keep your shop safe.

- Follow manufacturer's instructions for every piece of equipment.
- Don't work when you're too tired. If selling your work starts pressuring you to jeopardize your safety, it's time to reevaluate your motivations.
- Wear safety glasses or goggles whenever you're in the shop.
- Protect against hearing loss by wearing protective earmuffs. Racal Health & Safety, Inc., of Frederick, Maryland, makes a combination eye and hearing protection system for $28 that includes impact-resistant spectacles that can be worn with or without protective earmuffs.
- Avoid repetitive stress injuries by avoiding projects that require hours of making the same motion over and over. Take frequent breaks when projects do call for repetitive motion.
- If you don't really need a power tool, don't use it. Hand tools generally create less dust, less noise and less danger. So, if a job can be done almost as quickly with a non-power tool, use it.
- Protect yourself from wood dust. This is such an important issue we'll give it its own section (below).
- Have a fully stocked first aid kit readily available.
- Again, get and use the *Woodworker's Handbook*. It covers how to safely operate every major piece of woodworking equipment.

More on Dealing With Wood Dust

Wood dust can cause dermatitis, respiratory irritation, allergic reactions, asthma and nasal cancer, according to the National Institute for Occupational

PHOTO BY HAL WOOD

Wood-carver Bob Hawkins shows a dust-collection hood he built to use with high-speed grinding tools in his basement workshop. A hose leading from the bottom of the hood to a vacuum cleaner in the cabinet beneath it collects the dust. An acrylic sheet positioned at a 45-degree angle facing Hawkins lets him see his workpiece and protects him from dust. The slanted back helps direct dust toward the dust-collection hose.

Safety and Health. The link between wood dust and lung cancer is less strong, but a concern nonetheless. In a poorly ventilated shop, wood dust can also be a fire hazard.

A respirator or dust collection system isn't an extra, it's a must for a healthy workshop. Protecting yourself from wood dust doesn't have to be particularly expensive. Masks can prevent most of the dust from entering your air passages. And portable respirators that cost under $100 can do an even better job for prolonged exposure. But they don't solve the problem of wood dust in the rest of your shop.

Dust collection systems mounted to each machine are expensive and generally impractical for home shops or individual artisans. Since you seldom use more than one machine at a time, a portable dust-collection system that's strong enough to handle the output of the biggest tool in your shop is the best idea.

Generally, that means a unit that handles up to 400 cubic feet per minute (cfm) of airflow. Such a unit can accommodate home-shop tools such as a table saw up to 16″, band saw with blade up to 2″, jointer up to 12″, surface planer up to 20″, or belt sander up to 12″ wide. Most home-shop lathes take a bigger unit with at least 500 cfm capacity and sometimes up to 880 cfm or more. Larger belt sanders and shapers may also require 1200 or 1600 cfm capacity, respectively. With several portable models on the market, you can handle loads of 1200 cfm or less for around $300. To approach 2000 cfm capacity, you'll have to spend $500 or more. A larger capacity than you need right now is probably a good idea, because you may want more powerful machines that need more capacity later.

For wood carvers, dust collection can be a somewhat easier process. Several portable models are available that fit on grinding tools. Or, you can make your own dust-collection hood for power grinding, using a small dust collector or converted vacuum cleaner to suck in the dust.

CHAPTER ●Checklist

DETERMINE WHAT EQUIPMENT YOU REALLY NEED
- ☐ Stationary power tools
- ☐ Hand-held power tools
- ☐ Non-power tools
- ☐ Specialty tools

FIND EQUIPMENT SHORTCUTS
- ☐ Use accessories to get your tools to do other jobs
- ☐ Start a tool/shop co-op
- ☐ Outsource some work

CUT LUMBER COSTS
- ☐ Avoid using exotic species
- ☐ Use plainsawn or flatsawn rather than quartersawn
- ☐ Use found wood

CONCENTRATE ON SHOP SAFETY
- ☐ Follow manufacturers' instructions on all equipment
- ☐ Don't work when you're overtired
- ☐ Wear safety glasses and ear protection
- ☐ Minimize repetitive motions or take frequent breaks
- ☐ Use power tools only when you have to
- ☐ Protect yourself from dust with masks and dust collection systems

Shop Smarts Help Woodworker Raise Price, Lower Costs by a Third

After quitting his job as a manager for a security firm in 1990, Ray Murray was looking for a new career. Chance turned him into a woodworker.

Ray Murray discusses pricing with a client in his Cincinnati workshop.

"In all honesty, I knew nothing about wood—absolutely zero," Murray says. "But a friend of mine owned a rental store and told me the bunk beds he was getting were junk. He asked me if I could build him a set. I did, and I sold it to him the same day."

That was the beginning of what would become The Wood Works, a shop outside Cincinnati that now has sales of more than $400,000 a year. Murray finds his success in woodworking a little mystifying, but he chalks it up largely to the sales ability he developed during twenty-two years in the security business. A choice location doesn't hurt, either. The Wood Works is located on U.S. 50 east of Cincinnati with a traffic count of 22,000 cars a day.

But another element in the shop's success has been the sourcing savvy Murray has developed through trial and error. When he set up shop, he sold bunk beds for $199, while paying only $97 for the materials. Today, Murray sells bunk beds for $299 and up, but materials cost him only $67. Better craftsmanship accounts for the higher prices, Murray says. And smarter buying learned through trial and error has led to the roughly 30 percent reduction in material costs. Among the buying steps Murray took: reducing spending on ⅜″ plugs from $.05 apiece at a local builders' supply store to two for $.01 in lots of 5000 from a local dowel manufacturer. Murray also reduced his cost for dowel rods from $2.39 to $.35 apiece by buying direct. He found the manufacturer's address listed on the side of a box at the builders' supply store. He cut his cost for stain from $21 to $13.99 a gallon by soliciting bids from local paint and hardware stores. He bought sanding belts for $.70 apiece from a flea market vendor and lumber direct rather than from lumberyards. "I was paying $.65 a board foot for No. 3 pine," Murray says. "Now I can get No. 2 for half that." He has similarly reduced his cost for red oak from $3.19 a board foot to $1.19.

Convincing the lumber suppliers to bypass retail channels required minimum orders of $200 and some arm twisting, Murray says: "They said they wouldn't sell to me at all, because I wasn't a big enough business and I was already buying from their retail customers. I said: 'I bet Howard Ain (a local television news ombudsman) would like to hear that.' " After that, Murray says the wholesale suppliers became more accommodating.

Finding Your Niche in Crafts

here are thousands of niches to fill and thousands of ways to fill them. Your edge may be your ability to finish a piece of new furniture so that it looks 300 years old. Or you may have a source for beautifully figured boards that few others know about. Perhaps your years as a bird-watcher have given you a knowledge of bird behavior or physiology that few other wood carvers can match.

What You Do Best

Beginning woodworkers are usually generalists. Trying a lot of different projects is the only real way to find out what gives you the most satisfaction. After several years of woodworking, you're more likely to know what you like to do best, which is probably what you're best at.

The easiest way to develop a specialty is to start with your background and what you like to do. If you're an antique buff as well as a woodworker, antique reproductions are a natural niche for you. If you can gets lots of hardwoods unique to your area, you can specialize in furniture or turnings made from such wood. Look to your other hobbies, your job, your childhood experiences or education for inspiration.

Quality Beats Quantity

Another important consideration in choosing your niche is looking at competition from mass-producers—full-time wood shops that turn out lots of things fast. The furniture industry centered around High Point, North Carolina, is an obvious example of such competition. But lots of smaller shops making a variety of items are included in this group, too.

Big woodworking shops have some unshakable economic advantages over individual artisans. They can buy wood in volume, use their own kilns, buy the fastest computerized machines, and incorporate production line processes for added efficiency. If you try to take them on head to head, you'll likely end up banging yours against a stone wall.

Generally, such mass production shops crank out thousands of pieces annually, make a relatively small profit on each piece, and charge prices you could never make money with if you made the same piece yourself.

As an artisan, your approach has to be different. Your strategy is to make relatively few, high-value, high-profit items. You increase the value of your work by making each piece more valuable, not by making more pieces faster.

Here are a few considerations in choosing high-value niches that bypass or overcome competition from the big boys.

- *Quality.* Can you make things better than what's mass-produced, and are people willing to pay for it? Maybe you can make a TV tray better than a factory, but does anybody really care? On the other hand, some people in your town may be willing to pay the price for a set of Windsor chairs handcrafted from hardwoods native to your region and made to last a lifetime.

- *Originality.* Can you make something unique and find the clientele interested in it? Something that appeals to one in 100,000 people may not justify the overhead for mass-producers. They don't want to risk a big run for an untested item. Yet, such an item could be a great market for you. Keep in mind that an idea doesn't have to be new to work. If you can discover some long forgotten but still interesting craft item, you may be able to develop it into a modern-day money-maker.

- *Image.* This is less tangible than the other factors, but still important. Many people are willing to pay more for something handcrafted. It means a lot to them to link a name or a face to something in their home. If you have a compelling story behind your work, that enhances your work all the more. One disturbing trend in recent years is mass production shops passing themselves off as artisans at craft shows. Some reportedly are doing this even at shows that officially forbid such trickery. These "Mom & Pop" operations may have sales representatives posing as artisans and manning booths at two or three shows in different cities on the same weekend. Such tactics are unfair. But they do at least point out that you, as an individual woodworker, have something mass-producers consider valuable enough to try ripping off—your image.

- *Flexibility.* Mass production is for a one-size-fits-all world. But one size doesn't fit all, especially for some items. Entertainment centers, occasional tables, computer tables and office desks are a few such things. Your ability to do custom work and take the time to really get to know your customers gives you an edge over big producers.
- *Authenticity.* Mass-producers can knock off thousands of Queen Anne chairs. But their authenticity is usually a little suspect. You may be able to base your work on a superior knowledge of period furniture or accessories, making reproductions so close to the original it would take an expert to tell the difference.
- *Artistry.* Mass-producers can't make one-of-a-kind art furniture, carvings or turnings. If your work is truly a work of art—an individual expression—you've got a market all your own.

Looking at these factors, it's obvious some items lend themselves better to production by artisans than factories. Turned burl bowls, none of which are ex-

actly alike, are clearly in the artisans' realm. Several other woodcraft items that are more easily mass-produced can mean stiffer competition for artisans from big woodworking shops. Here are some areas where it's most important to keep competition from big producers in mind when you design your products.

- *Jewelry and hand mirrors.* You can't compete in the very low priced items, but some craft shops report demand for distinctive items—such as mirrors with finely crafted handles—that they just can't seem to find.
- *Picture frames.* Again, if you make distinctive frames that aren't easily mass-produced, you can still make sales here.
- *Kitchen utensils.* Wooden spoons and forks need to be pretty distinctive for you to compete. But wood mixing bowls, salad bowls and sets (with forks and spoons for tossing) could be a more promising market if you can find a way to produce them at a reasonable price. Craft retailers report trouble finding more utilitarian wooden bowls, as opposed to decorative turned wood bowls. An advantage with cutting boards is that they can be made with scrap pieces. The disadvantage is that big producers have a lot more scrap around than you do, and often use it to turn out low-priced cutting boards.

Making Child's Play Pay

In a world of putrescent fluorescent plastic action figures, there will always be a place for traditional wood toys. Kids may not go for them anymore, but their beleaguered parents will.

The wooden toy and game niche is a craft show

Bird Trainer Turned Bird Carver

Love of birds has led to both sides of a dual career for Gary Denzler, a world-champion bird carver from West Harrison, Indiana.

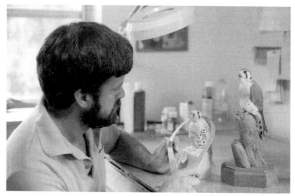

Gary Denzler makes a clay prototype of each carving before starting to work on the wood. Then, he uses calipers to transfer the proportions to his block of wood before carving.

Denzler's day job is as bird trainer at the Cincinnati Zoo and performing live bird shows at Paramount's Kings Island near Cincinnati. Throughout the summer, he puts on shows featuring tricks he has taught his birds to perform. Denzler's show is one of only a handful in the U.S. featuring free-flying birds. In one show-stopping trick, a hawk released from a platform more than a hundred feet above the stage swoops down and lands on his shoulder on command.

Since Denzler works six days a week throughout the summer, he earns enough compensatory time off for his second job as a professional wood-carver. When he's not caring for and training his show birds, Denzler spends his winters creating bird carvings in exquisite detail.

His carvings are good enough to have earned first place in the professional class of the 1988 Ward Foundation World Championship Wildfowl Carving Competition in Ocean City, Maryland. The prize netted Denzler $5000 and a push toward a second career that now pays as much as his first one.

Denzler owes both careers to his keen interest in birds and some help from friends. As an admittedly shy grade school student, he spent countless hours after school watching birds in a huge wooded city park that bordered his backyard. In the course of his bird-watching, he met a park ranger and photographer who specializes in photographs of birds in the wild. With the help of this friend, Denzler's knowledge of birds grew by leaps and bounds over the coming years.

At seventeen, fresh out of high school, Denzler saw an ad for a job at the zoo. Telling the zoo director of his longtime love for birds and animals, he talked his way into a job as a caretaker in the ape house. After a stint in the Navy and assignments in other areas of the zoo, Denzler became a full-fledged bird trainer in 1982.

Denzler's second career followed a less direct path. He got interested in carving after he admired a porcelain hawk in a Virgin Islands jewelry store during his honeymoon. When he saw the price, he realized he'd have to make his own bird figures if he ever wanted to own any.

Back home, he found a fallen piece of white pine behind his house and tried his hand at carving. He carved an eagle, which he describes as a crude piece of work for which he used a soldering iron to burn in the feathers.

"But people saw it and encouraged me," he says. "I started making stuff for people, and it just took off from there."

Denzler's carving wouldn't have gone beyond occasional pieces for friends, however, without help from one of the nation's top bird carvers.

After seeing the work of seven-time Ward Foundation winner John Scheeler in a magazine in 1985, Denzler sent him a letter and a picture of one of his carvings. He was amazed to receive not a letter, but a phone call inviting him to visit Scheeler in New Jersey.

Packing a few belongings and one of his show hawks in his pickup truck, Denzler drove to meet Scheeler. From that meeting, he learned techniques and got encouragement that rapidly turned his hobby into a profession.

"After that," Denzler says, "He [Scheeler] would call me once a month to find out what I was working on." Scheeler encouraged him to enter the amateur class of the Ward contest, which he won in 1986. Denzler then took third in the professional class in 1987 before winning in 1988. Denzler says he never would have entered the contests, much less won them, without the help of Scheeler, who died in 1987.

But Denzler also owes much of his wood carving success to the intimate knowledge of birds he's developed over the years. Being able to bring live models home from work doesn't hurt. Nor does the fact that he gets plenty of photos from his photographer friend to research projects.

"If you're careful and get the bird's head turned in a natural way, it makes it so much more lifelike," Denzler says. "I want the head to be cocked, for instance, like it's looking up at something. When you do that with the head, everything changes. All the proportions (of the head, in perspective) change."

Some carvers try to do the trick by sawing the head off the carving, then reattaching it at the right angle. "When you do it that way, it looks like that's what you did," Denzler says. "I used to do it that way myself, so I know."

Besides exhaustive research on each project, Denzler makes clay models before starting on the wood. He then transfers the proportions to the wood using calipers. The process ultimately saves him time and wood, he says.

Denzler's renown for wood carving earned him another project in which he reversed his usual process. He landed a commission from the Cincinnati Museum of Natural History to make sixty-eight fiberglass birds for an exhibit. For that project, he used wood carvings of some birds to make the clay molds that in turn were used to shape the fiberglass birds.

and craft shop staple that includes everything from low-priced whirligigs to high-end hobbyhorses and more. One advantage for part-time woodworkers is that wood cost for such small items is low, and many toys can be built with scraps from larger projects. Labor is a relatively large part of the price, meaning the potential for profit from your efforts is good.

Unfortunately, the competition is plentiful. Toys lend themselves to mass production fairly easily. Differences in quality of workmanship are relatively hard to spot compared to many other items. Stores specializing in wood toys and other baby items have sprung up in suburban strip shopping centers. While these stores may present market opportunities, they

Top 25 Most Popular Wood Items in Craft Shops

Below are the results of a national survey reprinted by permission of *Woodshop News*. The 100 craft shops participating in the survey were asked to name their most popular woodcraft items. The results are ranked according to the number of times a craft store owner mentioned the product.

You can consider this table in several ways: If something is popular, there must be a good market for it; or, if that many people are already selling boxes, why should I get into it? The best approach is probably somewhere in between. Boxes may be great sellers because of their popularity, but your items must be different from, and better than, the competition, and there should be enough unmet demand in your area. Keep in mind, too, that the table only accounts for craft stores. It doesn't include furniture stores, mainstream gift stores, or some other specialty stores that can be good markets for your work.

Rank	Item	Number of Times Cited
1.	Wooden boxes, jewelry boxes	57
2.	Occasional tables (end tables, coffee tables, plant stands, etc.)	28
3.	Kitchen utensils (cutting boards 12 times)	24
4.	Turnings (total) Functional bowls (13) Decorative, sculptural bowls (8) Vases (2)	23
5.	Clocks	21
6.	Desk accessories (pens, letter openers, card holders, etc.)	15
7.	Picture frames	13
8.	Bedroom set/bed	9
9.	Dining room set/table	8
10.	Rocking chairs	8
11.	Mirrors (wall and hand)	8
12.	Shelving	7
13.	Chairs	7
14.	Toys/games	6
15.	Chopsticks	6
16.	Birdhouses	4
17.	Kaleidoscopes	4
18.	Office furniture, desks, computer desks	4
19.	Earring holders	3
20.	Marquetry pictures	3
21.	Carved birds/animals	3
22.	Wine bottle holders	3
23.	Stools	2
24.	Bookcases	2
25.	Entertainment centers	2

also present plenty of ready-made competition. Also, mail-order houses now sell low-cost patterns and kits allowing woodworkers to easily make an amazing selection of games and toys.

All these factors make originality and creativity especially crucial in the toy and game segment. Inventing new wooden toys and games or retrieving old ones from an obscure local heritage is one way to approach this niche. Tailoring toys directly to adults can be another successful strategy.

Boxes, Birdhouses and More

Though small in size and price, knickknacks can be a big market for woodworkers. Among these items, boxes are perhaps the biggest opportunity. Their appeal is universal because the price is usually low and almost everyone can use a wooden box to store something.

A big plus for craftsmen is that boxes can be individualized so many ways. Box makers need never make the same box twice thanks to size, shape, style and design possibilities.

Here are a few styles ranging from the tried and true to the unusual.

- Simple dovetailed jewelry boxes
- Shaker oval boxes
- Band saw boxes
- Artistic or sculptural boxes
- Boxes based on architectural themes (patterned after classic buildings, etc.)
- Toy chests
- Russian-style "nesting" boxes (boxes within boxes)

The price range is as varied as the boxes themselves. Simple jewelry boxes may sell for as little as $15 or $20. Intricate designer boxes by California architect-turned-woodworker Po Shun Leong range as large as 6 feet tall and sell for as much as $12,000.

Birdhouses: No Longer Just for the Birds

One of the emerging markets for woodworkers in recent years has been birdhouses and feeders. Once strictly utilitarian objects, birdhouses have become much more varied, colorful and popular. Stores specializing in birdhouses and other supplies for attracting and feeding wild birds have sprung up across the country. Art and craft galleries now carry "artistic" birdhouses, some of which are so finely crafted that their owners keep them inside. More traditional retail garden centers and hardware stores are also good markets for birdhouses and feeders.

Though traditional-style birdhouses and feeders sell well, originality appears to be the key to greater demand. And while people will pay good prices for well-built birdhouses, there's a limit. Pennsylvania woodworker Barry Leader, for instance, saw sales of his Victorian-style birdhouses, priced $200 to $1,000, plunge dramatically. So he reworked his entire line, emphasizing funky and humorous designs—from cats to open mouths to colorful painted patterns. He also lowered his prices to $90 to $140. The result was a resurgence in sales.

Frills get sales, but the utilitarian nature of the product can't be overlooked. Some people may buy the houses as indoor accent pieces, but most hope to attract birds. Birdhouse makers study birds and their habitats, which allows them to tailor houses for individual bird species.

Miniatures: Small Market With Big Potential

Dollhouses are an enduring toy for children and adults alike. Though they can be mass-produced, there's still room for the artisan who can handcraft truly unusual houses—detailed right down to their wainscoting and gingerbread trim. Some sell for as much as $25,000, unfurnished, to collectors.

Potential also lies in furnishing the houses or otherwise creating original miniature reproductions. Collectors have paid as much as $1,000 for miniature furniture with microscopic dovetails.

Archiblocks Build Monumental Sales

What started as a small idea in a small studio turned into monumental sales for a Vermont woodworker in 1988.

Archiblocks, which are sets of maple building blocks in classical Greek and Roman architectural styles, started as a casual suggestion that filtered down through hearsay. They took shape on a lathe in Ron Bower's basement shop. Today, they're a million-dollar-a-year business for Interactive Arts in Vergennes, Vermont, the company to which Bower ultimately sold the business.

"They happened quite by accident, like most ideas do," says Bower. He had been a potter most of his life and had only recently redirected his efforts to making wooden walking sticks with tops turned on his lathe. One day, soon after Bower's career shift, his wife had a chance conversation with a neighbor who is an art consultant. The consultant was to have a meeting with a buyer for several museum shops nationwide, and she mentioned that the buyer was lamenting her fruitless efforts to find Froebel blocks.

Froebel blocks are children's building blocks in classic architectural styles. Milton Bradley once made an American version of the blocks, but stopped decades ago.

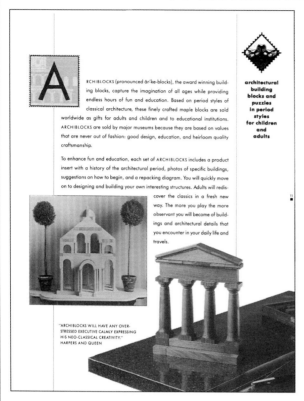

"ARCHIBLOCKS WILL HAVE ANY OVER-STRESSED EXECUTIVE CALMLY EXPRESSING HIS NEO-CLASSICAL CREATIVITY."
HARPERS AND QUEEN

Bower's catalog grew to include other wood products on architectural themes, such as Architectural Vignettes, which are maple boxes containing two- and three-dimensional architectural art. Archiblocks grew from a whimsical idea and a basement lathe into a million-dollar-a-year business for Ron Bower and Bower Studios. He ultimately sold the business.

The blocks were first developed by Freidrich Froebel, the nineteenth-century German educational reformer, who, after dropping out of architecture school, also invented kindergarten. Legend has it that Frank Lloyd Wright's mother gave him a set of Froebel blocks when he was a child in hopes of inspiring him to become an architect. Apparently it worked.

When he heard of the conversation, Bower decided to turn out his own versions of architectural blocks between other, more serious projects. He started with Doric columns, then moved on to other Greek and Roman styles. He also made arches and pediments with his band saw. He started stacking the blocks upstairs on his kitchen counter as he finished them. "This went on for about two weeks, until my wife was about to throw me out of the kitchen," Bower says. "At that point, the light bulb sort of went on, and we thought we had a product here."

Bower shot slides of his blocks in April 1988 for applications to juried craft shows in the fall. Though he hadn't fully developed the idea, he decided to go ahead with the applications anyway. In the meantime, a toy company found out about the idea and Bower negotiated licensing the product to them. After three months of negotiations, however, he decided he could market the blocks better himself.

"That summer and fall, I went into the basement and did the first 500 sets by hand," Bower says. "I took them to three retail craft shows to see what would happen, and they were a runaway success."

With money he made at the retail shows, Bower went into full-scale production. He contracted with several manufacturers to produce the blocks. Then he turned his efforts to developing packaging and catalogs to show wholesale buyers.

By January, he was ready to approach the market full tilt. He set up a booth at the New York International Gift Fair, the nation's largest wholesale craft exhibition. Successful sales there led to national distribution in time for the Christmas season of 1989. A favorable review of Archiblocks in *The New York Times* helped ensure success that first year.

Sets of the maple blocks in Greco-Roman and Gothic styles retail for $29 to $338, ranging from a forty-seven-block "Desktop Sampler" to the 107-block "Master Russian Collector's Classic" with acrylic case. Store owners who've sold the blocks say they appeal at least as much to adults as to children, and they are a particularly popular desk accessory for architects.

"Although building blocks are certainly nothing new in the world," Bower says, "nobody really seemed to be doing them with a complete architectural flavor—namely, period-style blocks."

Archiblocks led to several other related woodcraft products on architectural themes from Bower Studios. In 1990, the company started selling Collapsible Classics, a line of furniture made from lacquered, high-density particle board, with silk-screened takeoffs on Roman and Greek architectural details. In 1991, Bower introduced Architectural Vignettes—modular maple boxes that contain two- and three-dimensional architectural details reminiscent of 19th-century dioramas. They're decorative "sculptures" that can be placed on walls or desktops.

Bower has sold architecturally inspired Christmas ornaments, bas-relief wooden puzzles and Archiboxes—containers with architectural-style lids. And he has custom designed pieces for corporate clients based on their own buildings. The possibilities—and the sales—are seemingly endless.

Miniature woodworking is big enough to have spawned its own suppliers of tiny tools and mass-producers of miniature moldings, window sashes, siding and other millwork. But because of the unusual skill involved, miniature woodworking is dominated by individual artisans and families.

You don't even need to furnish a whole dollhouse to make money with miniatures. Nic and Linda Nichols, a Point Pleasant Beach, New Jersey, couple, make "room boxes," furnished entirely in miniature period furniture.

Other Original Creations: A World of Possibilities

- *Clocks.* Mass production of grandfather clocks, plus the tremendous amount of time and material they can take, makes this end of the market a tough one to crack. Many mass production grandfather clocks use glass liberally to cut down on cost, so all-wood clocks can be a niche that attracts discriminating buyers. The wider range of lower-priced wall and table clocks can present a better opportunity. The key, again, is

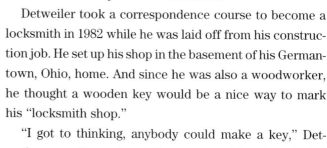

Woodworker Has Lock on Originality

A construction worker and contractor by trade, Tim Detweiler is a tinkerer by nature. That tinkering led to a lucrative sideline making working wood locks that would one day become his career.

Detweiler took a correspondence course to become a locksmith in 1982 while he was laid off from his construction job. He set up his shop in the basement of his Germantown, Ohio, home. And since he was also a woodworker, he thought a wooden key would be a nice way to mark his "locksmith shop."

"I got to thinking, anybody could make a key," Detweiler says. "I wondered if anyone could make a lock." He built a 16-inch high working wood padlock, the first of four he made to decorate his shop and home. Everything in the locks is wood, including the springs. They work essentially the same as metal locks, though Detweiler simplifies the design.

"They're such a conversation piece that a few people said if I ever made one to sell, they'd be interested in buying one," Detweiler says. He started making them for friends and later started selling

Tim Detweiler displays some of his wood locks at an Ohio craft fair. Each lock is made entirely of wood, including the springs.

them at craft shows. Even though the locks are fully functional, customers use them for show rather than protection.

Detweiler has used pine, cherry, walnut, oak, birch, mahogany, cedar and even such exotics as purpleheart and zebrawood. "Anything with good contrast to it works well," he says. "People like the hardwoods because they're a little more colorful when they're finished."

The large locks Detweiler made at first took so much wood that he felt he'd need to charge $500 to $1,500 for them. "I figured no one is going to buy one that costs that much, so I started toying around making them smaller—right down to a miniature one." He found that his savings on the material for the smallest locks was more than offset by the increased time needed to do the work. So he compromised by selling a version that's 8 inches high.

Detweiler originally sold his locks for $29.95, except for ones made from curly-figures burls, which went for $69.95. As his reputation grew, he raised his prices to a minimum of $40 and now sells most locks in the $40 to $60 range. He has sold some larger, more elaborate locks for as much as $800.

To price his locks, he drew on his experience in construction contracting, figuring in everything from an hourly rate for himself to the cost of sander belts and electricity. Wood cost was a tricky item at first, because Detweiler started with a supply of oak and cherry he had kept in his shop for twenty years and worked out in trade at that point. So he used current market prices.

The locks are durable by any standards. "I've made more than 600 locks over the years, and in that time I think I've only had three sent back because they didn't work," Detweiler says. "They worked when I tested them, but a little wood shaving got into the works later on." Detweiler will fix any defective locks and return them free of charge. "The demonstrator I use at my table [in craft shows] has been used for two years, and it's made of softwood," he says. "I tell people I wish I had a dollar for every time somebody has opened it."

On the craft show and festival circuit, Detweiler has seen other craftsmen who make wood locks, some even working versions. But he's found no one else who makes working locks from 100 percent wood. The closest anyone has come is a lock with everything but the spring made from wood. Not surprisingly, Detweiler keeps how he makes those springs a secret.

Though Detweiler has stuck with regional shows, he has attracted customers from New York, California and Germany. One New York locksmith placed an order after reading about Detweiler in an antique lock collector's magazine.

After being laid off again in 1991, Detweiler had decided to turn lock making into a full-time occupation. He geared up for enough production to meet what he projected as a strong Christmas demand. But then he got called back to work. Four years later, however, he "retired" for good and turned his lockmaking into a full-time retirement career. To keep his social security from being reduced, Detweiler has incorporated his business. The corporation pays Detweiler a salary that equals the maximum a social security recipient can earn without penalty. Any other earnings from the business come to Detweiler in the form of dividends from the corporation. As dividends, they don't count against the amount he's allowed to earn under social security.

Making his hobby into a business hasn't hurt Detweiler's enjoyment of it any, he says. "There's nothing much to watch on TV anymore," he says. "So every chance I get, I just like to go down to the basement, turn on the console stereo I have hanging from the joists, and let my troubles go—taking it out on the wood."

finding ways to make your product as original as possible.

- *Instruments*. You likely won't get far in violin making without years of specialized training. But other traditional instruments have been good sellers for individual artisans. Dulcimers and flutes are among the most popular instruments sold by woodworkers, and frequently show up at top craft fairs. To do a creditable job, you almost have to play the instrument you make so you can learn how to create the best possible sound. Some dulcimer and other instrument makers supplement their sales by selling recordings of their own music or that of others.

Probably the best potential sales opportunities are the ones no one has come up with yet. The world of unusual knickknacks and bric-a-brac is almost limitless. Here is where your unique background comes into play. You can draw on your job, other hobbies, your heritage, hometown, or any experience as a springboard to craft a novel item. The secret is finding some nook in your background that will also hook other people into buying your product.

Band Saw Boxes to Beat the Band

This fish box is 14″ long and 6″ deep and stands 12″ high.

Steven Martin started with a commonplace concept and made it as distinctive as possible. The result is a one-man craft business that's lasted fifteen years and gets better all the time.

Band saw boxes became popular in the 1960s. As the name implies, they're made by using a band saw to carve out pieces, which are reassembled into something that looks like a jigsaw puzzle, only with drawers, hinged lids and hidden compartments.

"I use logs, which makes mine a little bit different," says the Carterville, Illinois, woodworker. "Most band saw box makers use lumber." Each of Martin's boxes is different because each log he uses is. The shapes of the logs dictate the contours of the boxes. Martin calls them "sculptural" boxes, because they take on the look of free-form sculpture—only with drawers. (These boxes have anywhere from one to twenty drawers, each with a lever and spring so they open when pushed.)

Martin's boxes are distinctive to his Southern Illinois-Ozark heritage, because they're made from native woods. His boxes are made from red cedar, walnut or sassafras with a Danish oil finish. Most of the wood consists of "found" pieces, though not necessarily found by Martin. Though he once scoured the forests himself for just the right trees or fallen timber, he has since found a logger to do most of the work for him. "I was really particular about what tree I could cut, and I got really good at recognizing the suitable trees, particularly in cedar," Martin says. "But that got to be so time-consuming." Now, Martin says, he works with a guy who owns a small logging company. "Every now and then he shows up with a truckload of things he's been holding back for me."

He still takes advantage of storm damage when he finds it, or gets timber when friends tip him off about someone who's removing a tree.

Martin doesn't use imported exotic woods because they rarely make it into the country in the form of logs that Martin could use for his style of boxes. Also, he believes using native species makes his boxes more distinctive. And environmental concerns about destruction of rain forests is making customers increasingly reluctant to buy products made from tropical woods.

Martin uses essentially the same techniques he started with part-time in 1977 and went into business full-time four years later. But in recent years his work and sales have developed further. "The boxes are a little more complicated now," he says. "I've got a lot more projections, points and decorative limbs coming out of the boxes. Before, they were just sleek contours. It seems to be more popular, though I don't know for sure if that's totally responsible for my increase in sales."

Most of his boxes now contain some kind of secret compartment—one of

This box is 22″ long and 8″ deep and stands 15″ high.

their most popular features. "That can make a sale right there," Martin says. "People are looking for places to hide something. It's appealing because it's secretive. It's appealing to me, so I can understand." Placement of the secret compartments varies depending on the shape of the log.

Martin sells about 80 percent of his boxes at the fifteen regional craft shows he attends each year, selling the rest through mail order or consignment sales at regional galleries where he places his work. He only goes to juried shows, which are those that accept only a limited number of artisans in each craft based on applications. He finds the buyers are more serious at juried shows and the overall quality improves the image of his work. He also limits himself to shows in the Midwest to reduce travel time.

Martin's boxes range from $15 to $500, depending on size and complexity. Average boxes run $30 to $40. "I've tried to keep them relatively affordable," Martin says. "I tend to lean toward wanting to sell and make more rather than selling less for a higher price. I think by trial and error I've reached a price where they'll sell."

CHAPTER •Checklist

FIGURE OUT WHAT YOU DO BEST

☐ Try a variety of project types; choose what satisifies you

☐ Look at what you like to do

☐ Look at what your region offers in supplies and opportunities

☐ Look at your hobbies, job, experience and education

FOCUS ON HIGH-VALUE NICHES THAT OVERCOME COMPETITION

☐ Quality

☐ Originality

☐ Image

☐ Flexibility

☐ Authenticity

☐ Artistry

Finding Your Niche in Furniture and Specialty Crafts

Going from hobbyist to pro in furniture making may seem tough. You can't produce furniture as cheaply as a factory. And it's harder to sell fine furniture through outlets that are readily available, like craft shows, than it is to sell lower-priced items. Difficulties aside, furniture making is where many artisans thrive. Their originality, finely honed skills and craftsmanship are the keys to their success.

Custom Furniture

This is one area where big shops compete poorly. Even if they make custom pieces, large shops don't offer the one-on-one consultation a small shop can. This market is based on craftsmanship and personal service. Pros get the most business, but there's no reason a part-timer can't get some of it.

Entertainment centers are one good source of custom work. As consumer electronics get more sophisticated, factories have a harder time producing entertainment centers that meet everyone's needs. As a result, some of the most popular custom furniture projects are entertainment centers made to fit a specific place and specific pieces of equipment.

Office furniture—particularly home-office furniture—is another area where custom furniture makers can thrive. Mass-produced office furniture just doesn't always fit the very specialized needs of some businesspeople. And even when it does, many executives are looking for a mark of distinction, or a way to add a personal touch to a coldly impersonal corporate office. Home offices are particularly likely to have peculiar space requirements that demand custom furniture. Though many home office workers outfit their space as cheaply as possible, some are far more lavish with their quarters than any corporation.

Personal computers are everywhere, and as systems become more varied and specialized, demand for custom tables or workstations is also rising.

The possibilities in this niche are as varied as the people who buy custom furniture. They include making reproductions to fill out dining room sets no longer produced by factories, made-to-order antique reproductions, high-end furniture design for upscale homes, even designer cradles and baby furniture.

But breaking into the custom furniture market can be difficult for beginners. The most natural way to start is by doing work for friends and neighbors who know you're a woodworker, and to whom you can suggest ideas. Otherwise, here are some ways you can get custom furniture sales off the ground:

- Establish a good reputation by word of mouth. Start with work for friends and family.
- Get to know interior designers, architects, store owners, builders and other furniture makers who may be interested in contracting your services. Rather than being your competitors, woodworking shops can be your best friends. Professional furniture makers around the country complain they can't find decent help. A few small cabinetmakers have realized they can fill gaps in their labor force by using skilled hobbyists as subcontractors. They benefit from trained labor without fixed overhead. The benefit for you is the chance to make money doing what you love and improve your skills at the same time.
- Put your work in front of the public at craft fairs. Even if you don't sell your custom work directly at the fairs, they can be a good way of making contacts with potential customers.

Custom furniture making involves a different kind of customer service than other areas. You may sell some types of projects in a few minutes to someone you've never met before and will never meet again. Making custom furniture usually requires spending extensive time with customers to find out what they want. And customers expect total satisfaction for the high cost of custom furniture. If you're not comfortable with this type of contact or such high expectations, this may not be the niche for you.

Outdoor Furniture

The demand for high-quality or unusual outdoor and patio furniture keeps woodworkers busy in this market. Because it may not need much finishing and can be made of less expensive wood, outdoor furniture costs less than indoor furniture and can be sold more easily through such impulse outlets as craft fairs and festivals. Small home and garden stores can also be good outlets. A few of the styles that individuals sell successfully include folding-frame chairs and lounges, Adirondack chairs, and bent willow furniture.

Antique Reproductions

Popularity and dramatic price increases for antique furniture have created a boom in antique reproductions as well. Furniture mills keep up with the trends and mass quantities of knockoffs. But that doesn't meet the demand for reproductions that are faithful to the quality and craftsmanship of the originals. The slender legs and spindles of Shaker furniture, for instance, fare poorly when combined with second-rate joinery and lumber. Factory-made furniture also can come up short in duplicating the finer details that give reproductions a truly authentic look.

Homework is one ingredient for success in this market. David T. Smith, a Morrow, Ohio, woodworker, worked his way from being a hobbyist to owning a $2-million-a-year antique reproduction business largely based on his hard work and scholarship. He scours the countryside for boards with unusual figures and premium size. He reads antique publications extensively for new ideas. And he roots through the basement furniture collections of art galleries to study how period pieces really were made.

Outlets for your work can include fine furniture stores and other specialty stores, interior designers or individual consumers. Customers may be willing to pay more for antique reproductions made by the skilled hands of a single woodworker than those made at a factory. As with custom furniture, they expect the highest quality and satisfaction for their dollar. Repeat business and referrals are your best sources of sales, so your work must be top-notch.

Art and Design Furniture

As stark contemporary and Scandinavian furniture went out of style in the 1970s, the door was opened for far more individualistic designs. The result was a boom in elaborate design and art furniture. The distinction can be fuzzy, but one rule of thumb is that design furniture puts the emphasis on function with style, while art furniture places more emphasis on making an artistic statement.

Design and art furniture are perfect niches for artists and woodworkers. They would lose all allure if mass-produced, and the market for them isn't big enough to justify large runs. But there are still plenty of outlets for such work, including direct sales to

Willow Furniture—New Bent on an Old Craft

Bent willow branches have been used to make furniture for farms and homes across the rural Midwest at least since the 1830s when cheap nails became readily available, says Greg Adams of Muncie, Indiana. But Adams didn't discover the potential of willow furniture until 1983, when he was selling handmade willow baskets at a craft show and saw someone else selling willow furniture. He tried making furniture pieces at home and turned them into a popular product line.

Adams is a child welfare department caseworker during the week. On weekends, he puts in another forty hours making and selling his willow furniture.

His business is strong, and he doesn't worry about too many other people competing with him. "If you go out and make Windsor chairs or small wooden toys," he says, "there are a zillion people doing that." But he knows of only a half dozen or so willow furniture makers.

That's probably because finding willow is harder than it sounds. You can't go down to the lumberyard and buy willow sticks. "It grows in the wild, and you just have to know the area," he says. "It's a little like finding gold. It's out there,

Indiana craftsman Greg Adams makes willow furniture, like this love seat, from willow he collects during the winter. He says finding and cutting the willow is often harder than making the furniture.

you just have to know where to look."

Adams says it takes ten hours for him to make a willow bench he sells for $300. "About two-thirds of that time is getting the willow and getting it ready to make," he says. "I've gotten to the point where I can find the willow pretty fast. It's not that hard, but it's very labor intensive. I've got to haul a truckload of willow to make anything." Travel and craft fair booth fees, which range up to $450, are Adams's main expenses. Material costs almost nothing, except for nails and plywood used to support some larger pieces.

While willow trees are pliable, the surrounding flora and fauna is less forgiving. Adams has braved snakebites, ticks and even irate blue jays in his quest for willow. "Winter is really the best time," he says, "because you don't get snake-bitten as much."

The woodworking is the easy part. Adams's tool kit consists of a hammer and a set of pruning shears. He bends the willow into place and quickly pounds in nails. He knows some other willow furniture makers who use mortise-and-tenon joinery instead of nails. "That just blows me away," he says. "I have a terrible time measuring. If I had to make a mortise and tenon to fit in there, and measure it all and put it all together, there's no way."

Adams spends most of his free time in the winter making furniture to sell during the summer. He makes most of his sales through juried craft shows he attends throughout the eastern half of the U.S. "I basically try to stay in urban areas," he says. "You get out in the country and people tend to say, 'Uncle Leroy can make that.' And they're right."

Adams also has developed consignment outlets at galleries in and around northern Indiana. "That keeps the cash flow going and keeps me from having to do thirty shows a year." Instead, he does about fifteen. Another source of business is from customers who've seen him at craft shows and have taken cards. "I still get calls from people who saw me at craft shows years ago," he says.

Adams tries to make the most of his time spent at craft shows. He builds chairs while he tends the booth between inquiries from customers. Not only does that let Adams make the best use of his time, but it also adds an element of showmanship. "People really do like seeing the pieces made in the booth," he says. "I see a lot of people at shows who sit and wait and sit and wait. That would drive me crazy. If I run out of willow or nails or forget my hammer, I go nuts."

individuals, upscale furniture galleries and stores, and interior decorators who custom-order pieces.

Jamie Robertson, a Lincoln, Massachusetts, woodworker, runs the gamut of techniques with his work. His "funky Shaker," or Shaker styles with elaborate marquetry patterns, are made from brightly colored veneers. His less radical "dog tables" are inspired by his dog Coco. The tables are versions of popular styles but inlaid with dog figures in contrasting woods around the aprons.

Restoration and Refinishing

This seemingly unglamorous aspect of woodworking can be a great niche for individual woodworkers. Even if you don't want to spend your life, or even all your free time, restoring and refinishing furniture, it can help pay the bills as a part-time venture. Individuals are the primary customers for restoration and refinishing, but decorators and antique shops may also need top-notch restoration work.

Wood Turning

Wood turning centers on a very specific piece of equipment—the wood lathe. Its products encompass everything from 25-cent napkin rings to unique burl bowls sold to collectors for thousands. Rude Osolnik, whose one-of-a-kind bowls and vessels transform wood turning into an art form in the public's eye, also has turned and sold about 150,000 candlestick holders in his lifetime.

More than almost any other area, turning welcomes novices with open arms. A lathe is relatively cheap; the basic principles of turning are easy to master; and, where the beginner's enthusiasm for cabinet making or wood carving could fizzle out months before the first real project is complete, turning can yield the satisfaction of a finished piece in a few hours. Not surprisingly, turning became popular in the time-strapped 1980s. And more than in perhaps any other area, skilled hobbyists began turning their work into cash to help pay for their hobbies.

Innovation and artistry are among the turner's most important tools for selling high-end pieces.

Mom Refinishes Antique Wood Boats at Home

The first wooden boat Debbie Jones and her husband Jeff bought was aptly named *The Money Pit*. "It seemed like everything we had on that boat cost us a fortune to do," Jones says. "We made a lot of mistakes, but the more you do, the better you get."

What started as a money pit eventually turned into a money-maker and a career for Jones, who now restores and refinishes antique wooden boats for other people as a part-time job. She works from her garage and driveway outside Oxford, Ohio, much of the year, allowing her to look after her two children after school. Since most boats are being used, not restored, in the summer, Jones has summers off to enjoy boating and being with her family.

Most of the boats she works on are power boats built after 1920, such as Chris-Crafts. Many collectors scour the countryside looking for boats. Well-tended vessels command a premium price. But collectors can make the biggest gains by finding boats that have suffered neglect yet can be salvaged. That's where Jones comes in.

Restoring the boats involves three main steps—stripping and refinishing the hull, replacing rotted wood planks, and varnishing. Not all boats need all three. A wooden boat that's faithfully varnished every two years often needs little besides engine maintenance.

After buying *The Money Pit*, Jones and her husband joined an antique wooden boat club in Cincinnati and started attending boat shows. At one of the shows she met the owner of a boat restoration shop.

"We were talking about boats, and he jokingly asked, 'Why don't you come to work for me?' I took him up on it," Jones says. After six and a half years working for the shop and being promoted to shop manager, Jones got the chance to work for herself.

A wooden boat collector had heard about Jones's work through friends. He came to Jones's house to check out a boat she had restored and asked her to do some work for him. Since he is an avid collector with more than a half dozen boats, he offered Jones enough work to go into business for herself.

Almost all these boats are made from mahogany, so any mistakes are costly. Like fine furniture, the hulls of these boats can be marred by power sanders. So they must be sanded by hand, a painstaking and painful task that Jones likes the least.

The quality of Jones's work is crucial to her success. "Your work has to be flawless for you to survive," she says, "because so many collectors are doing the work themselves and are able to achieve work comparable to the professionals." Like other boat restorers, Jones builds her reputation through her clients' successes. Many of them enter boats in shows. When other collectors admire them, they ask who did the restoration.

Such pieces run the gamut from rough-hewn burls to high-tech art pieces conceived by computer-aided design and painted with automotive undercoating. Yet the market for functional, utilitarian turned objects hasn't been dominated by mass-production shops as much as might be expected. Candlesticks or simple wooden salad bowls with only modest styling can be big sellers for the individual.

Wood Carving

Like turning, carving is an area that takes little investment in equipment and thus attracts many novices. In fact, it attracts so many that it's difficult to make a living at. Despite the large ranks of carvers, true masters whose work appeals to collectors still earn very good livings at it, either part-time or full-time.

The variety of carving is almost mind-boggling. It includes chain saw carvers and miniaturists, chip carvers and carvers-in-the-round.

Much carving is done on a purely speculative basis and sold at craft fairs or through shops and galleries. But some carvers with established reputations do commissioned work, either for collectors or companies seeking pieces to decorate lobbies and offices.

Carving niches that can work well include:

- *Bird carving.* Ranging from duck decoys to naturalistic painted songbirds, this subspecialty has gotten popular enough to spawn national magazines for carvers and collectors. Though thousands do it as a hobby, those who've mastered the craft, including detailed carving and painting techniques, make good money at it.

- *Wildlife carving.* Again, hobbyists abound. But the best carvers can make a living at it, supplementing their income by teaching others as well.

- *Decorative carving.* Bas-relief or chip carving for furniture can add the distinctive mark that makes pieces sell. Even carvers who aren't furniture makers can look for shops or individuals with whom they could cooperate on projects.

- *Sign carving.* Carved signs add a special touch to homes, residential complexes, churches, specialty businesses, even as entrance markers for cities, villages and townships. This is the one aspect of carving that crosses the line toward the utilitarian. As a result, it can offer plenty of sales, but it's often overlooked by hobbyists and even professional carvers. You can market sign carving services direct to home owners and businesses through ads, or try to contract with a sign shop that doesn't offer the service.

CHAPTER •Checklist

GET YOUR CUSTOM FURNITURE SALES OFF THE GROUND

- ☐ Establish a good word-of-mouth reputation
- ☐ Contract your services out to:
  - —Interior designers
  - —Architects
  - —Store owners
  - —Builders
  - —Other furniture makers
- ☐ Show and sell your work in fairs and shows

CONSIDER SPECIALTY NICHES

- ☐ Custom furniture
- ☐ Outdoor furniture
- ☐ Antique reproductions
- ☐ Art and design furniture
- ☐ Restoration and refinishing
- ☐ Wood turning
- ☐ Wood carving

Turner Turns Bowls Into International Fame

As an industrial arts professor at Kentucky's Berea College in the 1940s, Rude (pronounced Rudy) Osolnik pursued wood turning as a hobby. A quirk of fate transformed his hobby into a career that gained him national recognition as an artist.

PHOTO BY GLENDA TENNANT NEFF

Rude Osolnik's wood turnings range from decorative bowls that sell for hundreds of dollars a piece to candlesticks that sell for as little as $20 a set.

For his weekend turning projects, Osolnik would use scrap wood from a veneer mill outside Berea. In return, he occasionally gave the owner some of his finished bowls. A friend of the mill owner was a corporate gift buyer for General Motors' Buick Division. When he saw the uniquely shaped and figured bowls, the buyer thought they would be great Christmas presents for GM execs to give. The buyer contacted Osolnik and placed an order. He also photographed Osolnik and his wife and placed a card describing his work with each of the bowls.

As those bowls circulated as gifts, Osolnik began to gain national and international prominence. One of his bowls was a wedding gift to Queen Elizabeth and The Duke of Edinburgh from Eleanor Roosevelt. And in later years, his bowls have been placed in collections and displays by major art museums nationwide.

"For a turner to make it strictly on turning, he has to be very versatile," Osolnik says. "He can't make it on just one item." When Osolnik goes to craft shows, he offers everything from one-of-a-kind bowls (which sell for several hundred dollars) to more functional items like candlesticks, which sell in the $20 to $50 range. And he always displays at least one new item at every fair he attends. "You have to be able to broaden your area, because people who've bought one of your pieces don't want to buy the same piece as last year," he says. But a turner's product doesn't have to be new to sell. Osolnik estimates he's sold more than 150,000 of the tapered candlesticks he developed in the late 1950s. "If the piece is well-designed, the design doesn't become obsolete." Indeed, candlesticks "inspired" by Osolnik's design are widespread in gift shops today.

Inspiration often comes by accident. When Osolnik was on sabbatical in 1981, he traveled with his wife to Belize. A woman in a house where Osolnik stayed made flowers from dough with wire stalks. His wife started making similar flowers when they returned to Berea. But she needed vases to put them in. Osolnik, who was reading a book on Grecian vases at the time, was inspired to make small "weedpots." The weedpots quickly became a hit. Like most of Osolnik's pieces, the weedpots are simple and understated. "I try not to clutter the pieces with doodads or curlicues," he says. "I try to let the wood be the focal point."

Flower Carving Blossoms—Satisfaction Into Sales

Richard McKenzie saw his first set of carved wooden flowers at a woodworking show in Columbus in 1976. It was shortly after he had suffered a heart attack, and he was looking for a relaxing hobby. But he got so good at whittling flowers out of tree limbs that his hobby soon turned into a moneymaking venture.

Though Richard McKenzie sells his wood flowers, his real payoff is the enjoyment of whittling them and of meeting the people who buy them. He only charges $.50 a flower. But since he uses tree branches he finds or are given to him by friends, his costs are minimal.

The tools and techniques the retired, London, Ohio, parole officer uses are fairly simple. With a simple carving knife, McKenzie shaves away thin layers of wood from one end of a tree branch, rotating the branch as he carves with a sawing motion. He then snips off the flower with pruning shears, and the branch is ready for more flowers to be carved.

He spray paints the flowers, mounts them on florist wire, and they're ready for sale. Each takes only about a minute to finish, and he'll do as many as four or five dozen at a sitting. But when they're done, the flowers are good enough to have fooled more than one customer into thinking they're the real thing, McKenzie says.

His costs are small. He pays $26 for a box of florist wire that can stem about 2,600 flowers, and $5 for a can of spray paint that can paint about four dozen flowers. The wood, which is ash or sugar maple branches cut from friends' trees, is free.

McKenzie only charges $.25 a piece to friends and $.50 to the public at craft fairs and festivals. He also sells them through a craft retailer in nearby Berlin, Ohio.

All told, McKenzie has sold 40,000 flowers. His flowers have been used in weddings and funerals in addition to household decorations.

Most of all, McKenzie's enjoyment is his biggest return on the investment. "People tell me I don't charge enough," he says. "But I do this because I enjoy it and it's relaxing. What I like most is seeing little kids look at them with wonder. Sometimes, I just give them away to them."

McKenzie estimates he sells about 600 dozen of the flowers each year at craft shows throughout Ohio. Even with that many sales, he still might not do more than break even after paying booth fees if the rest of his family didn't also get in on the act. McKenzie's daughter paints features on wooden animal figures he cuts on his scroll saw. His daughter-in-law paints vases sold with some of the flowers. Another daughter makes baskets and his son makes wooden benches. All of them combine their goods and their efforts at craft fairs.

How to Show and Sell Your Work

Outlets for selling your work are almost as varied as the woodworking projects you can sell. There are options for everyone from beginners to seasoned pros. But deciding what customers to approach—and then how to approach them—is crucial for getting the most in return for the time and money you invest. The best choices depend on such things as what you make, your personality and how much time you want to commit to selling.

Before you start selling your work, take an inventory—not of what you're selling, but of yourself and your situation. You'll need to think about who might buy your work and why, and where to find them. You should look at who else makes the types of pieces that you do and then develop an image that helps you stand out from the crowd. And finally, you'll want to find the best way to spread the news about what you do. Let's look at each of these steps in turn.

Knowing Thyself

You'll be more successful and content if you can answer the following questions before you begin showing and selling your work.

- *What's your niche?* The choices you've made about what you make play a big part in how you decide to sell it. You sell toys in a much different way than you would art furniture. There may already be specialty shops devoted to the kinds of things you make, and approaching them may be the perfect answer. Or there may be just a handful of people interested in buying what you make, and you should approach them directly.
- *What's your personality?* If you like traveling and mingling with the public, craft shows may

be a good option for selling your work. If you're more introverted or would get agitated by the occasional difficult customer, selling your work to stores by mail or phone may be a better answer.

- *How expensive are your pieces?* High-ticket furniture items may not sell as well at craft shows, because they're not impulse items. You may still want to take your work to some shows for the public exposure, but you'll need to make other provisions to sell your work as well.
- *How much time do you want to spend selling?* If you want to limit the amount of time you spend traveling to or sitting at craft shows, selling to shops may be a solution. Finding other ways to generate orders you can fill from your home—such as advertising—is another way to limit travel time but not necessarily expense.
- *Who do you know?* If you already know shopkeepers who might be interested in your work, or you have lots of friends and neighbors or some other network interested in what you make, you have a ready-made market that shouldn't be overlooked.
- *Where do you live?* If you live in a densely populated area, it's easy to find any number of outlets nearby. You can choose craft fairs, stores or other outlets much more easily and economically. If you live in a more remote area, it may make more sense to use the phone or mail to sell your work to retailers, to advertise, to find a sales representative, or to travel to a few regional craft shows rather than trying to sell to widely dispersed stores in your area.
- *How much money can you spend?* If you have only a few hundred dollars—or no money at all—to spend on selling your work, that limits—but doesn't destroy—your options. You can seek free

publicity through newspapers. You can sell work at fairs or festivals with low fees. You can call some shopkeepers in your area to introduce yourself, then pack up your goods and bring them in to demonstrate. Then, you can wait for money from early sales to help pay for costlier efforts that will net you more in the long run. If you have money to spend right away, you can create more elaborate printed materials to mail to stores, and attend more distant or more expensive shows at the start.

Deciding Who Your Customers Are and Learning About Them

Many people define their customers as anyone who's willing to buy their work. But narrowing your focus will make your selling job a lot easier. Look at what you make or do and think about who would want to buy it. Identifying those people is the first step to finding them—and helping them find you.

If you plan to sell your work to shops, the shop owner or buyer is the customer you must impress first, not the ultimate purchaser of the piece. Fortunately, many of the same things please stores and shoppers. They both want originality, quality and reasonable prices. But just because they're both pleased by the same things doesn't mean you can always please both at the same time. Some woodworkers juggle consumer and trade selling successfully. But if you're serious about working with stores over the long haul, there are some risks in trying to do that.

Many storekeepers don't like their suppliers to compete with them. They're paying you a wholesale price that they must mark up to make a living. If you then sell to consumers at a price lower than their retail price at craft fairs or "out the back door" of your shop, that can cost the store sales and make it look like it's gouging customers. Some retailers have been burned by this so often they won't even buy from local artisans.

Not all store owners are averse to working with woodworkers who work both sides of the fence. However, some store owners actively shop at retail craft fairs to stock their shelves or to contact artisans they'd like to develop into suppliers. That's particularly true if you don't undercut the store's retail prices.

Your niche may be such that the consumer/retailer question is irrelevant. If you want to sell your refinishing services, for instance, you may want to start by approaching wood shops in your area to find out if they need help. Or you may want to offer your skills to other woodworkers. Some shops not only will buy your work, but also help you with ideas for items to make. If you're a good carver, local furniture makers may be interested in subcontracting your skills. In that case, it's easy to find them through the Yellow Pages or a local chamber of commerce directory. Or your market may be so specialized that the ordinary channels for reaching consumers wouldn't make sense. If you restore antiques or wooden boats, for instance, it makes sense to ply your trade through clubs or shows.

Learning More From Your Customers

After you've decided which general area is best for selling your work, you can learn more specific information about your potential customers. Your research can help you find out whether there's demand for what you do and what kind of work will sell best. Here are some basic ways to learn about people who might want to buy your work.

- *Ask your friends.* Friends and neighbors are a natural source both of sales and feedback on your work. Ask them what they like, who they think would like to buy what you make, or stores that could carry your work.

- *Ask fellow woodworkers.* If you're not already a member of a woodworking club or a club for your specialty, like carving or turning, join one. Some woodworkers may have sold their work locally and can tell you how they got started and who they approached.

- *Try some shows.* Put together a booth and some of your work and try selling at a local festival or craft show. See how people react. If they're interested, they'll talk to you, even if they don't end up buying. Use the conversations to find out what kinds of things interest them, how they feel about the price you're charging, etc. Taking a few sample items to craft shows can be a great way for even an established woodworker to find out about new items.

- *Ask stores for advice.* Owners and buyers for craft and gift stores are easy to approach. Just call ahead to make sure you're not coming at a bad time. Take some samples of your work and ask them what they think, whether they would sell it in the store and at what price. Ask, too, what kinds of items they *haven't* seen anyone making that they think would sell. Even if you don't end up selling through stores, the storekeeper may have years of experience with customers which can be invaluable input for you. As with consumers, keep information about the retailers you meet in a card file with basic facts plus comments about what kinds of items might

sell well to the store or other pertinent information you glean.

- *Read.* Publications like *Woodshop News* and *The Crafts Report* contain a wealth of wisdom on selling and other aspects of woodworking. Subscribing to both costs only about $30 a year—which is a small investment for what you'll get in return. Also read more project-oriented woodworking publications to find out what people are making already and inspire new projects of your own. You can also learn from publications aimed at your potential customers. If you make Early American-style furniture or accessories, a publication like *Early American Life* can provide a wealth of information on fellow craftspeople, trends and interests of your customers. Make a habit of browsing the newsstand at a bookstore that carries a wide selection of magazines to see what's new and popular in your specialty. Don't forget your local newspapers as a source of information about new stores or fashion and consumer trends. Being systematic can help. Keep a filing system of clippings from various publications.

Knowing Who Else Does What You Do

One overlooked part of getting ready to sell your work is knowing what other woodworkers already sell. It's an important step for deciding on your prices, distinguishing your work from what's available, and gauging whether there's too much competition for you to sell an item successfully. You'll need to do a little legwork to do this research. Fortunately,

Bird Carver Has Keen Eye for Customers and Market

Bob Hawkins spent fifteen years as a hobbyist learning the intricate craft of carving and painting wooden bird figures. Since he retired in 1981 to take up bird carving as a paying avocation, he's been studying his customers, too.

Cincinnati bird carver Bob Hawkins hones his sales approach as finely as he hones his carving knives. He knows many of his customers are collectors, and all of them expect originality. So he makes every new carving a little different from the others.

The retired telephone company executive from Cincinnati learned his market through years of interacting with customers at craft shows and festivals. Today, while he still attends shows, most of his business is conducted by phone with repeat customers or people who've seen him at shows and call to order a piece later. Hawkins also sells to galleries, though he doesn't actively seek that market. If they see him or find out about him and place an order, he'll sell to them. "One thing I don't do is place work in galleries on consignment," he says. "I feel like I can sell the work better myself."

Most of Hawkins's customers are collectors, he says. That's one reason his business seems fairly recession-proof. "In the two or three small recessions since I retired we've found, believe it or not, that our sales increase," he says. "It might be due to the fact that we're dealing with people who have a little bit more money. They may decide to put it into collectibles instead of investments."

One way to appeal to collectors is special skill. Hawkins has spent years perfecting his craft, learning just the right grinding tools to use and just the right paint mixes and techniques to give his birds a lifelike sheen. As with other top-notch nature carvers, one acid test for Hawkins's work is being accused by horrified fair-goers of killing and mounting wild animals, when, in fact, they're all wood carvings.

Hawkins's pieces include duck decoys, songbirds, miniatures and shore birds. Some of Hawkins's customers are such avid collectors that they want one of every new type of carving he does, because each carving is somewhat different from all the others. He says, "One of the pitfalls people fall into is to let the dollars get in front of the quality, so they start making repetitive pieces. People can spot that right away."

Coming out with new categories of carvings helps keep Hawkins's interest and that of his fans keen. In the late 1980s, he came out with miniatures—scale carvings of songbirds perched on logs or fences. The miniatures turned out to be one of his most popular items.

Hawkins's carvings range from $200 to $900, meaning he must appeal to serious collectors rather than casual buyers. But he still wants to keep his prices low enough to attract new customers. So he came out with a line of lower-priced shore birds for $200 in 1991. Because carving the legs and feet takes little time, the shore birds are faster and cheaper to make. Yet, they're still realistic looking and enjoyable for him. "After you've been doing this a while, you may find that your prices are getting a little high," he says. "You're still selling, but you'd like to be able to meet another segment of the public."

How Hawkins presents his carvings at shows is important for attracting collectors, because the carvings must project a quality image. Having the right kind and right amount of light is important. Sodium vapor lighting used in many convention halls for indoor shows can wreak havoc with the delicate interplay of colors and luster that make Hawkins's painted birds look real. So Hawkins brings several desk lamps with him to put his birds in the best possible light. Hawkins usually uses two 8′ tables to display his work. He'll put no more than twelve pieces on those two tables. He also sells acrylic cases made by a friend to shield the carvings, but limits the number of them on the table. "A lot of people approach the display with a flea market atmosphere, trying to get as much on the table as they can," he says. "The real buyers of my type of work want to get a good look at what they're going to buy."

Matching the mix of carvings offered at a show to the locale helps Hawkins sell more of his work. "We find that the birds that are most common in the feeders in an area are the ones that sell quite well," he says. "Often, people don't even know what they are. But they've seen them."

All of Hawkins's merchandising aside, most of his customers don't buy their birds at shows. But the shows are still important, because that's where new customers see his work for the first time. "We go through business cards like they were going out of style," Hawkins says. "Then you end up getting a lot of calls in October or November for commission work. For a while, I was so busy I was a year behind on commission work and I couldn't even take any more."

Before he ships a commissioned carving to a customer, Hawkins sends a photo of the finished piece for approval. When the customer accepts the piece, he still keeps one photo of it on file as an insurance record for the customer. Only once or twice has a customer rejected a piece. If so, Hawkins may work on another to suit the customer if desired. "If they don't want the carving," he says, "I know I can find someone who does."

you can do much of it at the same time you're learning about your potential customers.

- *Read.* Check Yellow Pages listings for craftspeople in your area. Read the woodworking and craft publications mentioned earlier for profiles on woodworkers and how they operate. Read magazines in your specialty for similar profiles and ads from woodworkers. Keep up with the local newspaper to look for profiles and ads.

- *Check out stores.* See if they carry any items similar to what you make and if artisan names or addresses are listed. Ask a craft store manager about the work you're interested in selling to find out if they know where to buy it. If they do carry an item similar to yours, ask how well it's selling and why (or why not). Try to get ideas for ways to make improvements. Find out if they have trouble keeping the item in stock, indicating a demand you can help meet. Also, check prices. You can figure the store paid the woodworker no more than 50 to 60 percent of the retail price. That can give you an idea of market prices for what you make.

- *Check out craft fairs.* It's easy to get in as a customer even if you can't get in as an exhibitor at first. Shows are some of the best indications of what's going on in the market. Products and prices are clearly displayed, and the artisans are right there ready and willing to tell customers about what they sell. Besides the craft fairs close to home, try some in other cities or regions, especially if you happen to be traveling anyway. You may find ideas that would transplant nicely to your hometown.

Projecting an Image

Selling crafts is very different from selling most other things. For crafts, the person behind the product may be almost as important to the customer as the product itself. "Customers want to know about the guy who made it," says Paula Gollhardt-Leighton, owner of the Beautiful Things gallery in Scotch Plains, New Jersey, and a past president of the American Craft Retail Association. "They're buying the artist as much as they're buying the art." You don't have to have an amazing life story to sell your work. That doesn't hurt, of course, but any information the customer knows about you and your philosophy adds

meaning to what you make. If your background has a direct bearing on the kind of work you make or sell—say being a bird trainer and bird carver—that's an especially interesting point. Whatever your background, however, finding a way to get that story in front of the public is important.

Think about what aspects of your life and personality have shaped your work. Quality and originality are something everyone wants for their personalities and their products. But is there something more specific? Do you have, say, five generations of woodworkers in your family? Then, adding a "Father & Son" (or "Mother & Daughter") motif to the image you project to customers might be a good idea. When you have a clearer idea of the image you want to project, think of a possibility for a business name and logo to help everyone remember it. Your logo could incorporate your craft, some unusual aspect of it, or your background.

You may have the artistic or advertising talent to create your own logo. If not, it would be worth the investment to go to a graphic designer or even a local advertising agency. Even a bad logo is better than no logo at all, because any logo helps fix your business in the consumer's mind.

That logo can become part of a package of printed materials that includes business cards, brochures and more. These leave-behinds should cover more than what you make. They should help convey your image to your customer by honing in on your background and how you make your work. For instance, if you handcraft candlesticks or toys from maple grown in your state, your brochure should say so. Tell customers about the custom-blended oil finishes you use. And incorporate photos of yourself working on pieces to give customers a feel for the handcrafted originality of what you sell.

Projecting an image is more than just having the

right printed material. It's an integral part of your entire sales effort. You can also project a strong image in your booth by the way you display your work. You can bring a piece of work in progress and a few hand tools to enhance your image as an artisan. You might even do some work on a piece at the show. Or you can use photos of work in progress to tell customers how a piece was made.

Getting the Word Out

By now, you've got a pretty clear image of your product, your customers and your image. These are the basics of your message and the audience you want to hear it. Now, it's time to start getting the word out. Here are some ways.

Business Cards

Every woodworker who has something to sell—or anyone else who has something to sell for that matter—needs business cards. They're one of the cheapest advertising vehicles around, yet one of the best. If you call on stores in person or by mail, you need a business card to leave behind. Even if you only sell direct to consumers through craft shows or other means, you still need cards. You can pass them out to folks who haven't made up their minds yet, or who know someone else who might like to buy from you.

Here's how to get the most out of your business card.

- Get it typeset or laser printed by a desktop publisher or printer. Some woodworkers prefer handwritten cards for their folksy quality. But more often, handwritten cards can look amateurish or just plain ugly. Get a typeface that suits the style of your work. A designer, a typographer—or a calligrapher, if you decide on a hand-

written look—can help. Your card should show the same quality and originality your work does.

- Make sure the text includes such basics as your name, your company's name (if that's different), address and phone. A slogan or tag line about you may help too. Include a list of what you make if there is room without it looking too busy. Or, for a little extra, you can print this information on the back of the card to make use of that space.

- All-text cards can do the job. But some kind of logo or graphic image usually will do more. You may be able to incorporate your logo into your name, which will save some space. Even if you don't have a logo, try to include a photo or drawing of what you make, which will help customers remember you.

- Consider color, but don't consider it mandatory. Color is commonplace on business cards these days. But for somebody in a traditional craft like woodworking, color isn't always necessary. In fact, most wood products show up well in black and white. Used poorly, color may do more harm than good.

- Buy in volume. You'll go through a lot more business cards than you ever imagined. Buy by the thousand, or whatever is the best volume deal.

- Scatter your cards far and wide. Always keep some with you. You never know when you'll find people or bulletin boards that could use your card. At craft shows, display your cards prominently in the booth. It lets customers know you're a pro.

Other Materials

Besides business cards, you may want to add other printed material to your stockpile depending on how many things you sell, where you sell, and how much money you can invest.

sMm

sculptural boxes

steven m. martin

Band saw box maker Steven Martin's brochure does its job well with little space or expense. It has a simple, clean design and an attractive picture of what Martin sells, which helps customers remember who he is after a show is over.

Almost every woodworker can benefit from having a brochure or flyer that gives background information. A business card can convey some of this information, but it can't carry the whole load. A simple one-page, folded brochure with the same quality and similar graphic motifs as your business card can do much better. Even if you do sell to both consumers and retailers, don't try to use the same brochure for both. Rarely do both groups need the exact same information. Trying to make your brochure fit both groups ends up making you look unprofessional to the trade and too slick or too greedy to consumers.

If you've generated much of a mailing list through your craft show or retail contacts, you may consider sending out a newsletter or flyer periodically. This is a good way to keep your name in front of customers and inform them of new items you've introduced. Lest you waste your money, each mailing should contain some actual news that may interest the recipient. Examples of such news would be a new product or new product information (ways to use, ways to care for, etc.), reduced price, promotional sale offer, or personal news that might be of interest, such as winning an award. Again, this should have the same look and quality of your other materials.

If you make several products, a price list or catalog might make sense. The price list can double as an order form and be inserted in your brochure and/or newsletter. Again, make sure you use different ones for retailers and consumers. Catalogs can be much more expensive, but you can reduce the expense with black-and-white photography. Some retailers prefer working with catalogs. If you have only one or two items or if you can visit in person and show photos, you may not need one.

Advertising

If you could place an ad for a few months in *Architectural Digest* or *Country Home*, you'd soon have all the business you could handle. Unfortunately, you might end up working five years to pay for the ad. But less costly advertising strategies may work just as well for beginners.

For beginners and smaller-scale operations, newspaper classified advertising is one fairly economical alternative. A simple two-line ad in the same place over several months can yield results. Even larger display ads in the classified section may not be beyond your reach, and they'll let you use eye-catching graphics that jump out from the grayness of a want-ad section. You may do best placing your ad in a community newspaper or a zoned edition of a metropolitan daily, at least at first. The cost is lower than an ad in a citywide paper, and you can target a manageable area of town. Even if you plan to advertise citywide eventually, you might test your ad's effectiveness in a cheaper community paper first. Find out how it works and make refinements before spending bigger bucks.

Higher-priced advertising in regional and national consumer magazines is a better bet once you're more established and have the resources to pay for the ad and deliver on the customer demand it generates. Such ads work best for woodworkers who have succeeded in craft fairs and are ready to move into higher-volume or higher-priced sales. Magazine advertising can work especially well if you find a specialized publication that caters to a very specific client base—such as a bird carver advertising in a magazine that targets collectors of bird carvings.

Another old standby that shouldn't be overlooked—the Yellow Pages. This is the first place most consumers turn when they're interested in buying something. Your ad may not reach the same number of readers as it would through other media, but you can bet almost all of those readers are in the market for what you have to sell. One drawback—you usually have to have a business phone line to advertise in the Yellow Pages. This alone can cost you $500 or more a year, depending on where you

live. The ad costs go on top of that. So this is not an inexpensive option.

Though TV advertising may seem out of the question for woodworkers—or any small business—that's no longer really the case. Rates on smaller local cable systems are surprisingly low and comparable to display ad rates in community newspapers. True, you have the added cost of video production. But this can be done fairly affordably with a local production house. Your commercial can be seen during local time on such networks as ESPN, CNN, Arts & Entertainment or any cable channel you believe potential customers are watching. Even more affordable is buying the "crawl" that goes under the local weather forecast on The Weather Channel.

Don't overlook outdoor advertising—because customers don't. A billboard is most likely out of your price range. But if you live on a well-traveled street and zoning codes will permit it, a sign in your yard or on your house or shop can be a great way to let people know about what you do. Likewise, you can use your car or truck as a roving ad for your business, if that suits your style. Flyers on public kiosks or bulletin boards are another very low-cost alternative. But because these media are cheap, they don't have the highest public perception. Counter that by having your sign or your flyers done in the most professional-looking way possible.

Whatever kind of advertising you choose, persistence is the key. Don't expect a flood of inquiries or sales the first time your ad appears. It may happen, but it's rare. It takes time to build an impression. Make sure you can make the financial commitment to run your ad at least three to six months, or you're probably wasting your time. If you haven't generated much response by then, it's time to rethink your approach or quit advertising. Even if your ad is successful, you may eventually want to quit. Your goal is to generate a customer base. Once you do that, word of mouth may take care of the rest.

Along with persistence, consistency is an important tool in making the media get your message across. This is another reason to get a catchy logo. No matter how often you change your ad over the years, keep the logo basically the same. Over time, your logo will be increasingly recognizable to customers.

Getting the Media You Don't Have to Pay For

Don't be too quick to reach for your pocketbook when you think about promoting your woodworking. The best things in life, and the best media, come free. In other words, don't start forking out to get your name and face in a box on the bottom of the page before you try getting better placement up top for free.

Getting publicity is a lot easier than it may seem sometimes. Unlike advertising, it's always free. Newspapers and magazines have a big appetite for human-interest stories. And woodworkers are quite interesting to their fellow humans. There's something about the woodworker's traditional craft that makes it all the more compelling in a high-tech age. The more compelling your own story and the more novel and interesting your product, the better chance you have to get publicity for it.

That doesn't mean you just walk into the editor's or TV station producer's office one day and tell them you're ready to have your story done. You need a press release as your messenger to convince them your story is newsworthy. Having some kind of news angle to peg your story on is one key to giving your press release a sense of immediacy that will get editors' attention.

Almost anything can be "news" if you handle it right. Did you just win a prize at a craft fair for best turned bowl? Perhaps you can highlight the fact that you recently did well at the Springfield Craft Fair and you'll be at the Peoria Arts Festival next month. Or maybe you're scheduled to teach dovetail joinery at a woodworking club's upcoming meeting, or you sold a carving to a local celebrity, or you just started selling a new line of 18th-century reproduction boxes.

Even if the "news" in your press release doesn't rank up there with the fall of communism, the news editor's nose for human interest stories will help him or her realize the reader value of your story. Exactly what angle will work depends on the needs of the publication you're targeting. So take the time to learn something about the publication. News value isn't always essential to attracting interest if the human interest part of the story is strong enough. A background press release that sums up your personal and woodworking background can also do the job.

Most press releases follow a certain format designed to make them easy for the editor or TV/radio news director to use. They should be on 8½″ × 11″ paper with margins of at least an inch. The date should go somewhere at the top of the release. So should a line that reads, "For more information, contact:" and another line with your name and phone number. The release should be no longer than two

This simple press release accomplishes a lot in one page. The header includes the all-important contact name and phone number. The headline tells the story succinctly. The dateline tells editors of papers that this is a local story. The first paragraph answers the crucial *who, what, where, when* and *why* questions. The second paragraph shows that this really was an important honor. The third paragraph provides important background information. And the fourth paragraph provides interesting personal information about Woody Masters. Note that this fourth paragraph also tells where he used to live, which helps make this of interest to editors in Connecticut, as well. The fifth paragraph isn't absolutely necessary, but some papers might use the quote.

Header

Header

FOR IMMEDIATE RELEASE

Contact: Woody Masters

(802) 555-1212

Headline

Masters Takes Top Honors at New England Craft Show

Dateline

Who, What, When, Where, Why

BURLINGTON, VT—Woodworker Woody Masters received the Best of Show Award Sept. 29 at the fourth annual All-New England Craft and Design Show in Hyannis, MA, for what judges termed his "novel and inspired" wood boxes.

The show draws top craftspeople from throughout New England, including 250 artists and artisans from six states. Masters's boxes won top honors among the 50 woodworkers, carvers and turners and among artisans in all classifications.

Background

Masters's boxes are miniature replicas of homes found in and around his hometown of Burlington, VT. Doors and windows of the boxes open to reveal hidden compartments. The boxes range from as small as 6″ to as big as 3′ high. Each is unique, and prices for his work range from $150 to $2,000.

Personal Profile

Masters, 45, has been a woodworker since he was about 12 years old and a full-time woodworker for the past six years. He quit his job as an investment banker in 1990 to devote his time to his craft and moved from suburban Greenwich, CT, to a 100-acre dairy farm outside Burlington.

Quote

"I feel honored to have been recognized in this way at one of the region's most prestigious shows," Masters said. "Given the quality of the others' work, I was surprised to have won. While I didn't really go into woodworking to win awards, at least the award tells me I must have made the right choice."

—30—

pages. If there's more to be told, wait for the reporter or editor to call. Stick to the facts, plus an interesting quote or two from yourself, and resist the temptation to try anything cute or gimmicky.

The release should look professional, but it needn't be slick or flashy. Editors get thousands of slick press releases a year, and resist those that contain more hype than news. They think that the understated, matter-of-fact ones are more likely worthwhile.

Your release usually should include a black-and-white photo to illustrate what's in your release—either you or your product or both. Unless you're a good photographer yourself, get a pro to do this. This photo may end up being used. Even if it's not, you need it to help get the editor's attention. Also get the name of the appropriate editor, either from the publication's masthead or by calling to find out. Address the envelope and the press release to that editor.

There are two main types of press releases you'll want to use. One is aimed at getting the newspaper or station to do a feature story on you and your woodworking. This is a one-shot deal. At best, you might get a publication to do a feature on you every ten years or so, if there's been a significant change in story angle over that time. The other type is a new product introduction or event-related release, which you can try to get placed every time something new comes along. The first one is the best for generating public interest in your work. But you can keep following up with the others, because they don't hurt, either.

One drawback to free publicity compared to paid advertising is that you have no control over when (or if) it runs. It could be a few days or several months later. Wait at least two weeks after you've sent the release to call. Then, ask the person you sent it to if they received it and if they plan to use it. If they

reject you outright, at least ask why. It could give you feedback that will help future efforts. If they express interest or are noncommittal, ask when they might do something in the least pushy way you can. Don't become a pest. If nothing happens after you call, wait at least a month or two before calling again.

You'll have much more luck with some publications than others. Community newspapers will give you the best break. Some have policies that almost every press release that comes in gets run in some form within three weeks or so. Your chances of getting a feature story are best here. Larger metropolitan daily papers aren't too hard to approach, either. Getting into the main sections of the newspaper may be hard. But if there's a zoned neighborhood section, your chances skyrocket. Magazines, especially national magazines, can be much harder to crack. But if your story is compelling enough, it's not impossible. Don't overlook specialty or trade publications, either. Some people think only their competitors will read about them here. That's not so. Retailers, collectors and other woodworkers who might want to buy your work also get these publications.

Reaping Rewards From Giving Your Work Away

Giving your work away for charity can help a good cause, provide you with a tax break, and create very positive publicity. Giving your work to a museum can put your name in front of every visitor to the museum. Giving your work to a toy drive or similar effort at least generates goodwill among the volunteers and others in the community you work with. Public radio and television stations are some of the best outlets for charity auctions, which can be the best promotional vehicle of all. They may have auctions once or twice a year as fund-raisers. The folks who donate goods or services to be auctioned—besides helping the cause—get plenty of free plugs on the air and a new potential customer down the road in the form of the highest bidder.

Word of Mouth: The Best Form of Advertising

No matter how you promote your woodworking, you won't go far without one form of advertising—word of mouth. Praise and referrals from old customers are the lifeblood of any business. Part of the strategy is very simple: Do good work, do what you promise, and otherwise treat your customers fairly.

For Jack McCarthy, a wood boat restorer who owns The Wooden Boat Shop in Cincinnati, making his customers succeed provides strong word-of-mouth advertising. Many of McCarthy's customers like to display their restored boats at shows. McCarthy's customers have won their class in the Midwest's largest boat show in Michigan in several recent years. "That's how you get nationally known," he says. "My wife and I go to most of these shows, too. It's a non-pressure sort of thing. People see these beautiful ma-

hogany boats, and they take my card. And when they run into their buddies in Tuscaloosa, Alabama, they say I saw this guy in Cincinnati who does wood boats. The next thing you know, we're going to Tuscaloosa to pick up a boat." McCarthy has drawn customers from as far away as Florida, New York and California. Among his customers was magician Doug Henning, who winters in Maine and bought an inexpensive boat from McCarthy that he restored himself with McCarthy's long-distance advice.

Here are some other ways to make sure your customers spread the good word:

- *Circulate.* Being at craft shows or contacting retailers can help generate word of mouth even when it doesn't generate customers. Someone may remember you or, better still, keep your card and pass the information along to a friend who's interested in what you do. Otherwise, let everyone you know, know that you're selling your work now, and ask them to spread the word.

- *Put your name on your work.* It will help your old customers, and anyone who admires your work in their homes, remember your name. Plus, it adds an element of old-world craftsmanship that's appreciated.

- *Ask your customers for referrals.* Ask the shops or consumers with whom you do business if they know of anyone who would like what you do. Then, give the customer a brochure to pass along or get permission to give the prospect a call yourself. Rather than waiting for word of mouth to spread, force the issue some by calling prospects and telling them you were referred by the friend.

Spoon Carver Stirs Up a Niche

When it comes to niches, Norm Sartorius has found one of the smallest ones in the world of woodworking. Sartorius is quite possibly the foremost spoon carver in the United States. Maybe in the world. Unfortunately, he's at the top of a very small group. That isn't to say the Parkersburg, West Virginia, spoon carver doesn't merit recognition. He sold a spoon to the Smithsonian Museum in 1993, has had his spoons exhibited in shows from Cambridge, Massachusetts, to San Francisco, and has a small but dedicated band of twenty to twenty-five collectors nationwide.

If you are still having a hard time considering spoon carving an art form or discipline worthy of its own niche in the world of woodworking, you probably haven't seen Norm Sartorious's spoons yet. They resemble turned bowls more than anything else in the craft world, and they have been featured in several shows of turned objects. The concept of spoons as art, however, is one many people have trouble wrapping their minds around, Sartorius says. "People at shows will say: 'This is beautiful, but do you really put it in your spaghetti sauce?' They're juggling that whole issue of use versus what its function is if you don't use it."

Sartorius, and his spoons, defy classification to the extent that they may need a new category. His work falls somewhere between carving and turning—and even does

Despite questions of form vs. function, craft fairs, galleries, and a small group of collectors keep Norm Sartorius busy carving his unique spoons.

occasional mortise-and-tenon joinery for some pieces. He is technically a carver. Yet his work looks much more like the stylized lines of bowl turners than the realistic sculpture of carvers. Indeed, his first big break came when his spoons were included in a show of turned pieces. Yet some top collectors of turned work aren't ready to accept Sartorious into their world. "There are some turning collectors who are utter purists," Sartorius says. "I've had some very well known turning collectors come through my booth and look at every piece thoroughly and compliment me— but it's not turned, so they won't buy it."

Ironically, Sartorius compares his own situation with that faced three or four decades ago by some now-renowned turners. "If you went to a really good craft fair 30 years ago, there would be turners, but they would all have popcorn bowls and salad bowls and maybe some platters. It would be hard to say you could find a really personal style. Then, through the work of all these now-famous people, turning became an art form. At every show there are several booths with turning only as an art object. But it took the public some time to come around. I think it's a parallel thing [with spoons]. I'm trying to get people to see that spoons can be one-

A 4″ × 5″ × 1″ blood-wood spoon by Norm Sartorius.

of-a-kind specialty pieces, that they can be kept in a special way, much as you would some other art or craft object."

Even if the public may be somewhat slow in coming around to the concept of art spoon carving, Sartorius believes he made the right choice in fully committing to his craft in 1989. He dropped everything but high-end spoons and letter openers from his booth. He kept the letter openers only so he would have a few less-expensive items to sell and allotted only a small area of the booth for them. Most of his booth is now set aside for showing one or two spoons.

"The idea was that if I'm going to get people to look at spoons differently, I'm going to display them as they would be displayed in a gallery," Sartorius says. "I'm not going to be grouping them with 10 or 15 right on top of each other. I'm going to show one or maybe two, nicely lit on a pedestal."

The display concept worked, Sartorius says, but he decided to take it a step further by helping would-be buyers envision how the spoons could fit into their homes. Hanging a spoon in a kitchen is the first thought for many. But that's often not appropriate for spoons that sell for between $250 and $1200. So Sartorius had a cabinetmaker friend build him a lighted display case for his booth—something to suggest that spoons can be displayed in a hutch, corner cabinet or similar prominent places throughout a home.

Sartorius's movement toward art spoon making was a gradual process. It began when the former Baltimore social worker, still "wrapped up in the 60s," decided in the mid-70s to move to West Virginia to live a simple, subsistent lifestyle.

With no prior woodworking experience, Sartorius signed on as an apprentice for a Salem, West Virginia treen maker—helping make letter openers, show horns, knife racks, canes, light-switch plates and kitchen utensils—including spoons. That apprenticeship lasted six months before Sartorius seized a chance to buy 25 acres of land even deeper in the countryside of West Virginia, this time in McDowell County.

While there, he earned a modest income making treen items that he sold at craft fairs in the region. "It seemed all along," he says, "like people paid more attention to the spoons than the rest of the stuff."

After six years living in the mountains—the last year entirely on his own—Sartorius found it increasingly lonely. Craft fairs provided some badly needed human contact—and to this day Sartorius prefers selling his work through fairs largely because it helps him maintain personal contact with his customers. It was at a craft fair during his stay in McDowell County that Sartorius met a Murray, Kentucky, woodworker, Bob Falwell, who took an interest in Sartorius's work and his plight. "He felt sorry for me and thought I was doomed up there on the mountain by myself," Sartorius says. "He started buying my spoons and telling me I should give them more attention, that this was something worth pursuing."

With Falwell's help, Sartorius did just that. Falwell sent him scraps of such exotic woods as koa from his ship, giving Sartorius his first chance to work with such species. Eventually, Sartorius took Falwell up on an offer to come work with him in Kentucky. Sartorius worked with Falwell as a sort of apprentice for 18 months, trading his work for shop time and attending craft shows exhibiting his own work. Falwell, a graduate of the School for American Craftsmen who formerly taught sculpture and furniture design at Northern Illinois University, taught Sartorius about the business and history of woodcraft.

Sartorius's work soon caught the eye of Horty Scheiber, owner of the Pro-Art gallery in St. Louis, who invited him to participate in a show of turned work along with such major turners as David Ellsworth. She also helped him price his work, which then topped out at only $250.

While still based in Murray, Sartorius also met his future wife, Diane Bosley, at a craft show, where she was showing stained glass. Sartorius moved back to West Virginia, this time to her hometown of Parkersburg. Bosley now works as a secretary for a vice president of an oil company and provides the family with predictable income and health benefits. Sartorius, besides carving spoons, is primary caretaker of their eight-year-old son.

Sartorius estimates he puts about 30 hours a week into spoon carving, making 30 to 40 spoons a year and grossing about $20,000 annually. "If I were working 50 to 70 hours a week like a lot of crafts people, I have no doubt that I could sell the work. I have more demand than I'm able to produce. But it really doesn't fit the balance of my life to approach it like that."

One Woodworker's Promotional Toolbox

Rob Stigler is a full-time professional woodworker with three employees, but his time-tested and diverse approach to selling provides some valuable lessons even for smaller, part-time efforts.

Rob Stigler has found seeing is believing for his customers. Having a room to show customers pieces he has made shows them the quality of work he can do. And it helps them get an idea of what kinds of custom pieces they'd like to order.

Stigler owns Stigler's Woodworks, a custom cabinetmaking operation in Reading, Ohio, near Cincinnati. He says trial and error has showed him how to improve his sales approach during two decades in business, starting as a one-man operation.

Repeat business and word of mouth gets most customers to make appointments to see Stigler and samples of his work. And the key to getting that kind of business is simply doing a good job and being dedicated to meeting the customers' needs, he says. But he doesn't rely solely on word of mouth and repeat business, he says, because it's not always enough to keep sales where he'd like them to be.

Other ways Stigler uses to get customers include:

- *Yellow Pages advertising.* He's tried advertising in local newspapers and magazines with little success, but found Yellow Pages advertising works best for him. He has steadily increased the size of his display ad until it's now an eighth of a page. Customers frequently cite the Yellow Pages ad when they call, he says. He feels a large ad builds credibility with customers unfamiliar with his work. One drawback, however, is the cost. The ad accounts for most of Stigler's $500-a-month phone bill. But remember—Stigler started small and worked to a bigger ad.

- *Persistence.* Persistence is important in advertising, Stigler says. The large Yellow Pages display ad didn't produce fantastic results the first year, but Stigler stuck with it and saw results improve in following years.

- *Consistency.* Despite one name change and four relocations over the years, Stigler also stuck with the same logo design in his ads, featuring a Queen Anne's table leg. He thinks that has helped build a recognizable image with customers no matter how many changes he's made in other aspects of the business.

- *Getting customer names and addresses.* Stigler has been an exhibitor at the Cincinnati Home & Garden Show for several years. But his first year, he had little success because he didn't have a system set up to collect the names of people who came through his booth. "People may take a card and say they'll come and see you, but maybe one out of 400 does," he says. In later years, he asked visitors for their names and addresses and followed up with a mailing after the show.

- *Mailings.* Besides mailings to home show visitors, Stigler also keeps a list of visitors to his store and another of past customers. He keeps the three lists on an Apple computer and sends mailings targeted to each several times a year.
- *Showroom.* Stigler operates a small showroom next to his workshop as one key sales tool. Most of his customers call ahead to make appointments, Stigler says. The showroom isn't so much a way to introduce casual shoppers to Stigler's Woodworks as a way to show these serious shoppers what Stigler can do. Even though Stigler's is a purely custom shop, most of his customers don't know exactly what they want when they walk in the door. A few carry pictures clipped from magazines. But most have little more than a rough idea, or at best stick-figure drawings or a list of dimensions. Looking at display pieces helps Stigler define options for customers and show what he's capable of making. A showroom may be beyond the means of many beginners. But having a brochure, a photo album of finished pieces, or a few sample pieces you can show in your home can help do the same job.

CHAPTER •Checklist

TAKE INVENTORY OF YOURSELF
- ☐ What's your niche?
- ☐ What's your personality?
- ☐ How expensive are your pieces?
- ☐ How much time do you want to spend selling?
- ☐ Who do you know?
- ☐ Where do you live?
- ☐ How much money can you spend?

LEARN ABOUT YOUR CUSTOMERS
- ☐ Ask your friends about what they like
- ☐ Ask other woodworkers
- ☐ Try some shows
- ☐ Ask stores for advice
- ☐ Read related publications

LEARN ABOUT YOUR COMPETITION
- ☐ Check the Yellow Pages for local craftspeople

- ☐ Read publications for craftspeople profiles
- ☐ Check out stores
- ☐ Check out shows and fairs

PROJECT AN IMAGE
- ☐ Tell your story
- ☐ Project your personality
- ☐ Create a logo
- ☐ Create promotion items

GET THE WORD OUT
- ☐ Business cards
- ☐ Brochures, flyers, newsletters
- ☐ Price lists, catalogs
- ☐ Advertising
- ☐ Media releases
- ☐ Charity donations, pro bono work
- ☐ Word of mouth

A Guide to Ways and Places to Sell Your Work

Once you have a general idea of how to sell your work, you'll want to look more closely at exactly where to go next and what to do once you get there. This chapter is intended to help you find specific outlets available for woodworkers and ways to approach them to improve your chances of success.

Woodworkers use retail craft fairs and wholesale shows to sell their work. Retail show customers will almost always be ordinary consumers and collectors. Customers at wholesale shows are buyers for retail stores or other trade outlets, such as buyers who specialize in obtaining gifts for corporations.

Retail Craft Fairs

Woodworkers sell through retail shows for reasons that range from the enjoyment of traveling and meeting new people to being able to keep a larger share of the sales price than selling to retailers permits. Hobbyists who are starting to sell their work find shows are one of the best ways to get their work in front of the public and find out how it will sell. And even experienced full-time woodworkers make a substantial part of their income from retail craft shows. Whatever the reason, you should do some shopping to pick the best show for you. Here are some factors to consider.

- *Proximity.* Though some full-timers travel to shows nationwide, most part-time woodworkers try to stay at least within their region.
- *Attendance.* Some woodworkers say they can count on a sale for every thousand or two thousand attendees—some far more than that. How many sales you make per thousand depends on your price range and the mass appeal of what you make. You'll only find out by experience. But

at any rate, the larger the attendance, the better your chances.

- *Quality.* Raw attendance figures can be deceptive. The "quality" of the attendees is important, too. A general fair or festival with no admission charge and lots of food and entertainment offerings may attract hundreds of thousands of people. But most are there to eat or see entertainers, and only a small fraction to buy crafts. A much smaller craft show that attracts serious buyers could yield much better sales. Some shows devoted only to woodworkers may draw a crowd more interested in what you have to sell.

Several guides listed in the appendix of this book give details about shows, including such things as attendance, booth fees, sales figures of attendees, and comments or ratings by craftspeople who've been to the shows in the past. Also, your state arts council or local craft guild or co-op may publish a more localized directory. You also can get current information about shows, dates and times, and requirements for exhibitors from classified ads in *The Crafts Report.*

Here are the main types of shows you can choose from.

- *Festivals and fairs.* One plus is that these festivals and fairs are abundant in many parts of the country. They can be a good way to approach the tourist trade in vacation spots. And they're easy to get into if you're inexperienced on the craft show circuit. Festivals and fairs can be a good way to test how the public responds to your work—whether they buy it or not—before you take the trouble to get into shows that may be farther away, costlier and harder to get into.
- *Mall shows.* Some malls hold art and craft shows one to four times a year. Many of these shows

are sponsored by national companies, mall management or local clubs. This is one avenue for a local woodworking club to pool its efforts to show members' work in a retail setting (without taking as big a chunk of the price as a retailer would). The down side is that the crowd may not be particularly interested in buying crafts, but only came to the mall for other things.

- *Retail arts and crafts shows.* These shows concentrate on crafts and charge admission. As a result, most people who come through the gate are fairly serious about buying. The downside is that they often charge higher booth fees than fairs or festivals, plus they may charge a share of your sales (perhaps 5 percent).

- *Juried exhibitions.* These are the cream of the arts and craft shows. Exhibitors must have their work approved by a "jury" of artists, craftspeople or others designated by a company. The juries make their selection based largely on the quality of your work, as demonstrated by three to five slides. Some shows are extremely competitive, with ten craftspeople rejected for every one accepted. And many general craft shows will limit the number of exhibitors in any one medium, such as wood, to get what they consider the best mix. Some woodworkers will only exhibit at these shows, because the quality of their fellow exhibitors helps them maintain a quality image. And these shows are the best vehicle for attracting serious craft customers. One disadvantage is that you may have to pay an application fee—usually $10 to $25—whether you're accepted or not.

The Show Part of Craft Shows

The quality of your crafts plays a big part in your success. But the second word in the phrase "craft show" is also important. Here are some ways to enhance craft showmanship.

- *Build a better booth.* Part of the research you do before you start selling your work is looking at the booths of other woodworkers and artisans at craft shows. Check with fellow artisans about what kinds of canopies work best for the weather conditions in the area. Local hardware stores or companies listed in the appendix sell a variety of canopies. Companies that sell canopies and accessories advertise in *The Crafts Report* and other publications for artisans, such as craft show calendars. Most shows have display units of $10' \times 10'$ or $10' \times 8'$, so keep that in mind if building your own. Shelves can help take advantage of vertical space. For indoor shows, carpeting can help by covering the ugly concrete floors in most exhibition halls. Often, carpets and basic tables can be rented from the show promoter, which relieves you of the burden of transporting them to the show. Keep in mind that fire code regulations will cover electrical requirements, and usually dictate the material that can be used in tablecloths in your booth. It's best to ask show promoters about these requirements before you arrive at the show. Otherwise, you may have to pay high prices to rent or buy these items from suppliers at the shows.

- *Create an inviting display.* Again, study how experienced exhibitors display their merchandise. Don't try to pile too much into your display area. But do try to bring enough inventory to keep the display looking full. Store any excess away from the display area. Though your work is the centerpiece of your display, some other additions can also help you sell. Besides business cards and brochures, you may want to display awards you've won or newspaper and magazine clip-

Teacher Learns the Art of Selling at Shows

Art teacher Larry Joseph has made selling wooden toys and children's furniture at craft shows something of an art itself. His family's part-time business, Timber Toys, makes each show a learning experience. Since Joseph made his first wooden toy for his son, Jason, in 1976, both Jason and Timber Toys have grown a lot.

Joseph and his family now make more than twenty items, including a rocking horse, cradles, high chairs, strollers, doll benches and desk-and-chair sets for $6 to $50. Working evenings, weekends and summers, the family has made enough to pay for a two-story, 85'×45' workshop and garage in the village of Prospect, Ohio. Reaching that level of success has meant learning the best ways to sell products and knowing how to develop products that will sell. Joseph has found juried craft shows to be the best vehicle for both purposes.

When he started, Joseph took his work from shop to shop trying to drum up interest and sold some that way. But he found that took too much time for too few rewards. "It really got to be a hassle," he says. "They were almost doubling the price we sold things to them for. Instead of letting the other guy have part of the time we put into it, we figured we might as well sell it outright ourselves."

Then, the family tried fairs and festivals but found they didn't provide enough sales for the time spent. It was also hard to keep jostling crowds from damaging the merchandise.

Finally, Joseph found craft shows to be the best way to reach consumers. He used a craft show guide published by the Ohio Arts and Crafts Guild, a branch of the Ohio Arts Council, which rated and provided information on shows. And he tried as much as possible to get into juried shows, where he found the most serious buyers and highest-quality artisans and promotion. It took time to develop the quality of work needed by the better shows, Joseph says. "But we got to the point where we want to be. We've got some big shows that may last up to two or three weeks. But we don't have as many little shows." The family now sells through eight shows a year, all of them in central and northern Ohio.

Most of Timber Toys' sales come at fall shows. But Timber Toys does attend one or two shows in the summer to raise enough cash to buy lumber and materials and help test new products. The family spends most of the summer making products for the fall shows. During the summer, Jason Joseph has been able to devote himself full-time to the family business as a summer job during breaks from school, and later from college. After Jason graduates, Larry Joseph plans to eventually retire from his teaching job and devote full time to his woodworking business. "Each year we try to introduce a couple of new things," Joseph says. Craft shows are his test markets, providing instant feedback through sales (or lack of sales) and customer reactions. But Joseph seldom relies on the results of just one show. Experience has shown him too many cases where an item will do poorly at one show and great at the next.

When introducing a new product, Joseph usually makes a limited run of thirty to eighty. He prices it based on the material cost and labor. But since he knows the family will get faster making the piece over time, he tries to factor that into the price. If an item doesn't sell well, Joseph rarely drops the price, because it's what he knows is necessary for a comfortable return. Instead, he may either phase out the item or find a way to make it less expensively.

pings about your work. Mounting these on lightweight foamboard makes them easier to display inside your booth.

- *Talk.* Don't just let your work do the talking. Greet customers with a smile and answer any questions that may arise or tell them about any item they may be admiring. Telling a customer how something was made can help explain its value. You needn't be overly assertive, which can drive people away. But do look for cues, such as lingering, which can be signs the customer wants more information.

- *Do some work.* Working on a piece in your booth can be a fascinating attraction. This isn't practical for everybody, of course. You may not be able to set up a lathe or a band saw in your booth. But you can carve, or do some hand sanding or painting. If you can't do the work in your booth, a poster that shows how the work is made might also draw interest.

- *Put on a show.* This approach isn't for everyone, but it can be quite effective. Don and Dawn Shurlow of Rhodes, Michigan, dress in costumes from the 1800s and put on a demonstration of their handcrafted wood toys at craft shows, which attracts big crowds.

- *Develop a mailing list.* Ask customers to sign up for your mailing list so you can let them know when and where you'll be exhibiting in the future. If you leave the sign-up sheet where it's easily seen and filled out, people who aren't interested in buying at this show may request future mailings. You may be able to find out what kind of pieces customers are most interested in buying or other demographic information if you keep your approach very low-key.

- *Watch what's happening.* Pay attention to what is and is not selling well for you throughout the show, not just what's left at the end. But be persistent; don't drop an item because it didn't sell well at one show. It may be your best-selling item at the next. After the fair or show, make a record of what products you offered, how many sold, and how much you charged. This will help you choose the best products to offer the next time.

Wholesale Shows

The primary way of selling crafts to retailers is through wholesale craft shows. But such shows are probably not the best way for individual woodworkers or hobbyists to approach the trade, at least not at first. These shows are in a whole different league from ordinary craft shows. All the attendees are shop owners or retail buyers. The entry requirements and competition to get in are more difficult than for even the better juried retail craft shows. And the standards for booth display and merchandising are different and higher. These shows often are held weekdays, and because of the cost and the higher volume needs of many of the buyers, it may not make sense for you to use this route.

But it isn't entirely out of the question. If you produce high-end, high-priced furniture, for instance, a wholesale furniture show might work. You won't come away with many orders, but you won't need to.

Although most hobbyists will find concentrating on quality, not quantity, to be the best approach, if your niche lends itself to fairly high-quantity production, such as jewelry boxes, toys or games, you might also benefit from attending wholesale shows. Sometimes hobbyists and small operations can take a somewhat production-oriented approach, making numerous copies of the same piece and assembling several pieces at a time from parts previously made rather than making one piece at a time. Even top-notch wood bowl turners sometimes supplement their income with production-type items like candlesticks. Selling wholesale often does mean sacrificing some originality. While each piece may vary a bit, wholesale buyers purchase in volume, though it may only be three or four pieces at a time. Make sure you can and want to make relatively large quantities of an item or several items before you venture into wholesale shows.

You generally only take orders at wholesale shows rather than selling merchandise, so you only need to transport samples, not your entire inventory. Yet, some woodworkers sell at least three to four times what they would at a retail craft show.

Shows run by American Craft Enterprises, Wendy Rosen Shows, Beckman's, Western Exhibitors and George Little Management are some of the best-known wholesale craft shows nationwide. But more local shows can be especially good for independent woodworkers. The classified section of *The Crafts Report* is a good place to find ads and contacts for wholesale shows around the country. Also, reports in *Woodshop News* can give you an idea of how woodworkers have done at some of these shows.

Selling to Retailers: Finding Stores That Want Your Work

To simplify your sales efforts, consider what type of stores are best for selling the type of work you do. Here are the types of stores you may want to target and the best ways to reach them:

- *Craft shops, galleries and specialty stores.* These are the best outlets for artisans' work. They specialize in handcrafted items and have a clientele that appreciates them. But since they don't fall into a simple category, they can be hard to find through such channels as the Yellow Pages. One source is American Craft Enterprises, which lists 700 craft galleries nationwide in its guide "Shopping for Crafts in the USA." This segment can include art galleries, craft stores and some gift stores. So try checking the Yellow Pages under all those categories.

- *Gift shops.* This is a much larger segment, but it includes everything from high-end gift stores to souvenir stands, novelty and greeting card shops. Higher-end gift stores are the most likely to be good markets for the artisans' work. But it all depends on what you make.

- *Museum shops.* You don't have to be Picasso to get your work in an art museum shop. These are among the best outlets available for fine, handcrafted merchandise. Though much of what a museum shop carries relates to the museum's collection, some of it is general gift merchandise. Woodworkers who've marketed through the shops say they offer a sophisticated, upscale clientele and are thus willing to take a risk on higher-priced or unusual items.

- *Furniture stores.* Chain furniture stores usually buy from large furniture mills through the corporate office. But many furniture stores are locally owned and operated, and this can be a good market for you. Even if you don't make furniture, you may be able to sell handcrafted wood items at a furniture store as accessories. Higher-quality, higher-priced stores are more likely to need your work than others. Even if they carry major national furniture lines, they may want work from local craftspeople to fill in other specialties or to do custom work. It never hurts to ask.

- *Antique stores.* Even though a store may specialize in selling genuine antiques, it might need some new period-style accessories, reproductions, or restoration and refinishing help. This can be a great niche market for a woodworker. Unfortunately, there are some unscrupulous antique dealers out there commissioning work from skilled reproduction specialists and passing it off as the real thing—often without the woodworkers' knowledge. Watch out for this.

- *Other specialty shops.* If you make bird feeders or birdhouses, for instance, a local bird shop or nursery might be better than a craft or gift shop. If you make outdoor furniture, a local hardware store or nursery might work. Analyze all the possible stores that could be interested in selling your product. Even farmers markets or specialty food stores make good outlets for some woodworkers.

- *Department stores.* This is a market of limited usefulness for the independent woodworker, but not out of the question. Major department stores get most of their craft and gift items through wholesale shows. But it's not impossible to contact them directly. Remember that there's more than one way to get your work into department stores. Some woodworkers have had luck building display cases or making accent pieces that are used in displays for merchandising clothes, housewares or other non-furniture items. In such cases, you may end up dealing with store merchandisers rather than buyers. Stores may pay to use your work in a display instead of buying it outright. But having your work in such displays can also help you build future business if the display includes a credit for the woodwork. This approach may work with non-craft boutiques and clothing stores, too.

- *Craft and antique malls and flea markets.* Though technically *you* are the retailer in these situations, these markets do offer a setting and foot traffic similar to a retail store. The choices in this area keep growing, including the Coomers nationwide chain of craft malls and the seemingly endless number of antique and flea markets. In each case, you rent a booth or stall from the mall or market owner and in some cases also pay a share of what you sell, much like a craft fair. These malls and markets can be a good way to get a lot of exposure. But the drawback is that you can generally only sell lower-priced crafts here effectively. And the overall quality at these outlets is often a little less than you'd find at many craft shows. While this may be a good place to start, your goal should be to move on to other channels.

Selling to Craft Retailers— Some Do's and Don'ts

Woodworkers and craft shop owners offer the following tips for selling your work to retailers.

- *Make your initial approach by mail.* Try a mailing that includes a catalog or brochure listing wholesale prices and showing your work clearly and attractively. The more professional-looking the print presentation, the better chance of a sale.

- *Follow up.* Retailers may receive hundreds or thousands of mail solicitations a year. Though some report buying from woodworkers who only solicited by mail, a follow-up phone call or visit will help you stand out.

- *Call before you visit.* If you're selling to a store in town, it's best to call before stopping by, just to make sure the owner or buyer will be there and that it's not too busy a time.

- *Try easing the risk.* A guaranteed return policy or a no-risk sample order may help convince a retailer he or she has nothing to lose by carrying your work.

- *Consider adding a toll-free number.* If you think you might sell to a significant number of out-of-town retailers, consider adding an 800 line. It's not that expensive compared to the potential sales, and it makes you look like a pro.

- *Know the shop or gallery you're targeting.* Country craft shops won't be interested in modern art furniture. And avant-garde craft galleries don't need Queen Anne tables. Whippoorwill Crafts, a store in Boston's Faneuil Hall Marketplace, sells only handmade crafts with all parts bought in the U.S., including screws and other hardware. Some woodworkers and others have had their work rejected for not following such guidelines. Try to find out something about the shop by visiting or calling before you expend more time and effort in selling to them.

- *Help with merchandising.* Help stores by providing them with information about yourself as well as the product. Some stores, like Whippoorwill, even place pictures of the artisan with each product and keep a notebook with résumés and newspaper or magazine clippings about them. Other stores may not want as much information. But all of them would like some kind of material with the product, even if it's only a business card with a few details. Information about how the piece was made or how to care for it also is appreciated. But some retailers don't want you to include your address and phone number with the work, for fear their customers will seek you out to buy direct.

- *Don't add packing and shipping costs.* Make the wholesale price the delivered price. Retailers don't like getting stuck with an unexpected cost. So make sure your price covers your shipping cost, too.

- *Consider getting a sales representative.* If you don't have time or don't want to bother selling your work to the trade, consider experienced craft sales reps who will sell your work on commission. They may be able to take your work both directly to stores or to wholesale shows. Finding craft sales reps can be difficult, since there's no directory. But you can work in reverse order—asking craft stores in your area for referrals to good sales reps they've worked with. The advantage here, obviously, is saved time and increased selling savvy from someone who sells crafts for a living. The downside is that by the time the sales rep and the store get a cut, there may not be much left for you.

The Best Ways to Reach Retailers

Most retailers buy crafts through wholesale shows, but that doesn't mean you have to exhibit at wholesale shows to sell to retailers. A retail craft survey by *Woodshop News* found 81 of the 100 craft retailers surveyed buy through wholesale shows. But 49 percent said they have bought through direct contact by craftsmen. And 91 percent said they would be willing to buy items that way. Here are the overall results of the survey question that asked craft retailers how they source items to sell in their stores.

Wholesale shows:	81%
Craftsmen contact directly:	49%
Word-of-mouth, chance referrals:	22%
Sales representatives:	13%
Retail craft shows:	13%
Juried application:	12%
Catalogs:	5%

Note: The total exceeds 100 percent because most shops use more than one source.

Outright Sale or Consignment— and Other Terms

Once you've found a retailer who's interested, it's time to talk terms. For you, an outright sale to a retailer with cash up front is the best possible deal. But that may not always be possible. A recent *Woodshop News* retail craft survey found 54 percent of respondents make outright purchases only. But 27 percent only bought on consignment, and another 19 percent did things both ways. If you insist on an outright purchase, you could be eliminating much of your potential retail market.

Under a consignment deal, the retailer takes almost no risk other than using shop space that might go to a better-selling item. As a result, you should get a better portion of the retail price than when the retailer buys the piece outright. You may only get 50 percent or less of the retail price from an outright purchase. But you might get 60 to 65 percent from a consignment deal. Keep in mind that terms may vary widely from retailer to retailer. A consignment deal may be the only way to get your foot in the door. If the store has never carried a high-priced item like yours before, this may be the only way you'll get a

store to take the risk. If you go this route, do at least get a contract that specifies you will be paid immediately after the purchase.

For an outright purchase, there's the matter of payment terms. An outright purchase on credit can be worse for you than a consignment deal. Many woodworkers and other artisans insist on getting cash with the order or on delivery. Larger retailers will seldom work this way, especially with new vendors. But craft store owners, who are more likely to understand your situation, are more willing to pay cash up front. Some craft stores may want to pay you with a major credit card. Unfortunately, it can be difficult and expensive for a hobbyist or part-time woodworker to get vendor status with a credit card company. The American Craft Council, however, offers a plan whereby its members qualify for vendor status.

There are some compromises between consignment and outright purchase that could help make both sides happy. One alternative is a money-back guarantee or return policy. You could promise to refund the retailer's money if the item isn't sold within a certain time—say three to six months. Such terms are common for larger retailers and vendors. Or you could set up a limited consignment deal that would lead to repeat business. Give the retailer the first item on consignment or, if it's a lower-priced item, as a free sample. Get an agreement whereby if the item sells, the retailer will purchase replacement merchandise outright.

Other Selling Options

Though retailers and craft shows are the main outlets woodworkers use, they're not the only ones. Here's a look at other options that can supplement or replace these routes, depending on your situation and needs.

Shaker Furniture Helps Build Workshop

Like the Shakers who inspire his work, George Tyo of Lake Lorelei, Ohio, never set out to make a lot of money. His sales have been sporadic and not always profitable, but they have let him pay to retool his garage workshop.

George Tyo shows off one of his signature Shaker-style clocks, for which he also developed the silk-screened face. The clocks were popular, but they didn't prove profitable for Tyo when he sold them through a craft retailer. Selling other Shaker furniture through the shop, however, has allowed Tyo to retool his workshop.

Like most weekend woodworkers, Tyo started with low-cost tools. After five years of selling Shaker furniture through a store outside Cincinnati that specializes in Shaker furniture and accessories, he upgraded almost every tool in his shop from Craftsman to Delta models, and bought some tools he didn't have before. Now, Tyo's shop includes a full complement of Delta tools, including table saw, jointer, planer and lathe.

Tyo began selling his work more by accident than design. He had just finished the frame for a Shaker rocker for his son's first birthday and was looking for someone who could help him cane it. His wife saw the Shaker shop owner on a local television show demonstrating chair caning and suggested Tyo get in touch with the store. When he did, Tyo not only got his chair caned but also got an offer to make some furniture for the shop.

"I didn't want to go beyond my ability, so I started out making clocks, which were pretty simple," Tyo says. The clocks, joined with sliding dovetails, had faces designed and silk-screened by Tyo. They were a hit, and he sold nearly two dozen.

"Then, I started making some of the bigger pieces," Tyo says. He made candlestick tables, coffee tables, wall shelves and end tables. They proved far more profitable than the clocks.

Tyo's sales were almost risk free, because most pieces he makes are already sold before he starts. Either the piece has been ordered to be put on sale at the shop or custom-ordered by consumers through the shop. But there are some risks. Tyo still keeps one table in his living room that he made for the store but kept after he was unable to arrive at a price with the owner.

Because the shop marks everything up 100 percent, that wasn't the only time Tyo has had a hard time making money on a project. Sometimes, especially on lower-priced items, Tyo can make little beyond the material cost if the shop is to price the item low enough to sell. Tyo has stopped making his signature clocks, for instance, because they netted him little more than a dollar an hour for his labor despite retailing for $300. "You have to like doing it," he says. "Because you're not going to get rich. If you were selling to individuals and could double your money, that's where you could make some money."

Sometimes the arrangements don't seem fair to Tyo, because he does almost all the work and gets little of the money. The shop owner faces little risk or investment in custom-ordered pieces but still doubles his money right away. Yet Tyo still appreciates the work he got through the store. After the store owner passed away, Tyo stopped making much work for sale, other than to friends. But the legacy of his sales is a shop full of improved tools.

- *Commissions*. Commissioned work, either from individuals or companies, is an important source of business for some woodworkers. Some commissions come from friends, but most will come from contacts you make elsewhere, including customers who see something you offer at a craft fair that inspires something else they'd like to see you make. Corporations may want to commission work to decorate lobbies or commemorate important events. Word-of-mouth advertising is particularly crucial in commission work. Asking current clients for referrals to prospects or suggesting commission work to past customers are good ways to make contacts.

- *Selling from your home*. If you sell through craft shows already, much of your business could end up coming from customers who have seen your work. If they want another look before they buy, it may help to set up a display area in your home. You could combine that with advertising in local publications to draw customers. Keep in mind that this option isn't for everyone. Few homes are in retail areas. And if you bring much traffic through, you could spark zoning complaints from neighbors. This is also a bad idea if you don't want to be interrupted by customers or if you can't find a good place in your home or workshop to display.

- *Direct mail and mail order*. If you have a mailing list of customers, you can get repeat business by mailing them catalogs or more informal brochures and price lists. Even hobbyists can use simple direct mail. Just put together a postcard to tell past customers the dates and locations of upcoming shows. The card can bring customers to the fair looking for you, or may even lead to commissions from people who can't attend. Or, you can mail past customers a small, inexpensive brochure before the holidays with a clip-out form for ordering or more information.

Some furniture makers use lists of local zoning or building permits or deed transfers to find potential customers. These are available from county or city municipal offices, and you can either buy lists or stop by and copy down information. Anyone who is moving to a new home is a candidate for new furniture. And you can use listings of higher-priced homes to find people who are more likely to want custom-built furniture. You don't have to send a mailing to everyone who buys a new home. You can just target people in your area or in the price range you think will work best for what you do.

A full-fledged, four-color catalog is an option that relatively few independent woodworkers use, because of the expense. Cooperating with artisans in other media may be a good way to do this more economically. By pooling your efforts,

Co-ops, Guilds and Membership Organizations

Artists and artisans around the country have banded together to form their own outlets. These groups set up craft shows, exhibitions and sometimes permanent stores in cooperative efforts to sell their work. You can find such groups in your area by contacting your state art council, usually located in the capital.

One of the oldest of these efforts is the Southern Highlands Handcraft Guild, based in Asheville, North Carolina, and covering parts of nine southern and Appalachian states. Founded in 1930, the guild has about 900 artisan members. It markets their work through four stores in North Carolina and Virginia. The guild also holds its Guild Fair craft show twice a year. Guild membership lets you sell work through the shops or the fair, but you still must negotiate with each shop's manager separately.

Woodworkers and other artisans can join the guild through a two-part juried application process. The first part involves submitting an application and five color slides of your work. Applicants who make it beyond that stage get an appointment to show five pieces of their work to the guild's board, which will vote on acceptance.

On a smaller scale, the Illinois-Ozarks Craft Guild puts together an exhibition each year of the best crafts from the region. The exhibit is usually placed on or near the campus of Southern Illinois University in Carbondale, Illinois. You can also try forming an alliance with craftspeople in your area for such a cooperative marketing effort.

Some local arts groups also offer members and others the chance to display through their nonprofit galleries. For instance, the Ann Arbor (Michigan) Art Association lets members sell their work through its gallery for a 40 percent commission. The work first must be accepted by the gallery director, who sees new work one day a month or by appointment.

Several states also operate nonprofit showrooms for artists and artisans with terms more favorable than selling your work through a private shop. These include the Vermont State Craft Center, the Mississippi Crafts Center, and the League of New Hampshire Craftsmen.

you can combine mailing lists and share production costs. Or, you can trade work with a graphic designer for work on the brochure.

You may also approach existing mail-order operations to sell your work. Some catalog operations buy through wholesale craft shows, though you can try to approach them directly. Others, like the woodcraft program at Berea College, Berea, Kentucky, are primarily geared toward selling products they produce, but also may accept work from others to fill in their line.

Birdhouse Maker Tries Other Roosts
Before Finding Best Place to Nest

Mary Anne Donovan has juggled the roles of artist, artisan and businesswoman gracefully as she's developed a new medium and market in recent years. The art school graduate and former director of admissions at the Art Academy of Cincinnati quit in 1986 to pursue her own artistic career full-time. Then, to help support her painting, she turned her hobby making artistic birdhouses into a money-making sideline.

"I started with things from our yard to attract songbirds and make presents for friends," says Donovan, who used some modest shop training from art school and a band saw in her attic studio to create the houses. "A lot of my friends are artists, and some of them started wanting to order more from me as presents for friends," she says. Before long, she had a bustling business without even trying.

Each of Mary Anne Donovan's birdhouses is a unique piece of art. Having grown comfortable with consignment sales as a painter, Donovan has had success selling her birdhouses on consignment through art and craft galleries, too.

Like any piece of art, each birdhouse Donovan makes is a little different. They're in what she calls "funky, post-modern" styles, including houses with giant multicolored wings and houses accented by found objects, such as wooden forks. The artistic bent helps Donovan distinguish her houses with customers. "If they're interested in collecting something, it's usually because it's unique," she says.

Donovan is as experimental in her selling as she is in her art. Donovan tried selling her work at two juried craft shows in Cincinnati. She did well at each show, selling fifteen of the nineteen houses she brought there for prices over $200, plus some lower-priced ceramic bird feeders. But she decided it wasn't the right outlet for her, mainly because she didn't want to devote a whole weekend at a time to selling her work.

So Donovan tried another outlet she was more familiar with as a painter—art galleries. A friend told her about an art and craft gallery in Green Bay, Wisconsin, that might be a good outlet. "The owner responded immediately when I sent slides of the birdhouses," she says. Donovan's houses became a hit with tourists from Chicago vacationing in the area. Donovan then approached art and craft galleries in Louisville, Kentucky, and Cincinnati, where she also received good responses.

Donovan agreed to give her hometown gallery sole rights to sell her work in the area. "I'm used to that kind of agreement," she says. "With galleries, it's important that there's either one source or at least you're clear on exactly what agreement you have. They get all the referrals from me when people call."

Donovan works with the galleries on a consignment basis, but on the condition that she gets at least $150 for every birdhouse sold. The houses retail for $225 to $275, depending on what the gallery operator thinks is the best price. Donovan used to sell more inexpensive clay birdhouses and feeders, which retailed for only $12 to $40. But because of the lower price, Donovan found it impossible to make enough money on them to justify her time. It was especially hard to sell them out of town, which meant absorbing shipping costs.

Interestingly, Donovan has gotten recognition from the art community for her birdhouses just as her paintings. Three of her houses graced the grounds of the Ohio governor's mansion in Columbus, having been selected for an artistic exhibition sponsored by the governor's office. "I thought I was doing something more commercially based, but I've gotten some compliments and recognition from fellow artists, which is really nice," she says. "They're not just schlocky stuff to make money."

CHAPTER
•Checklist

INVESTIGATE DIFFERENT TYPES OF CRAFT SHOWS

☐ Festivals and fairs

☐ Mall shows

☐ Retail arts and crafts shows

☐ Juried exhibitions

ENHANCE YOUR CRAFT SHOWMANSHIP

☐ Build a better booth

☐ Create an inviting display

☐ Talk to customers

☐ Do some work

☐ Put on a show

☐ Develop a mailing list

☐ Watch what's happening, for the reasons discussed earlier

FIND STORES THAT WANT YOUR WORK

☐ Craft shops, galleries and specialty stores

☐ Gift shops

☐ Museum shops

☐ Furniture stores

☐ Antique stores

☐ Other specialty shops

☐ Department stores

DOs AND DONTs OF SELLING TO CRAFT RETAILERS

☐ Make your initial approach by mail

☐ Follow up

☐ Call before you visit

☐ Try easing the risk

☐ Consider adding a toll-free number

☐ Know the shop or gallery you're targeting

☐ Help with merchandising

☐ Consider getting a sales representative

☐ Don't add packing and shipping costs

How Wood Carver Chisels Market Out of a Few Sales a Year to Corporate Executives

When David Monhollen gave up his job as a corporate sales rep to become a wood-carver, he wasn't dropping out of the corporate world. He just started approaching it with a chisel instead of a briefcase.

David Monhollen poses with one of his bird carvings, a realistic looking sharp-shinned hawk.

Soon after Monhollen opened shop as a professional wood carver in the basement workshop of his Crittenden, Kentucky, home, he found the usual avenues of arts and crafts selling didn't suit him. Instead of working galleries or shows, Monhollen sells more than 60 percent of his custom pieces to corporations and executives. The rest is commissioned by other private collectors. He also has a booth at an area boat show once a year as a way to expose his work to a group of generally upscale boat enthusiasts who might be interested.

The result—payoffs that redefine the high end for most wood carvers. Monhollen's minimum price for a piece is $1500, but he rarely sells a work for less than $5000. His highest price to date was over $100,000. He averages $15,000 a piece, making six to twelve sales a year.

Monhollen had been a sales rep for Fortune 500 pharmaceutical and aerospace companies after he got out of college. But he had been carving since he was eight, and his mind often wandered to what he really wanted to be doing. "As the years went by, I figured I could do this when I retired," he says. "But this is like a magnet, it won't let you go."

"Everybody told me I was nuts," Monhollen says. Fortunately, he also got plenty of support. His wife, a teacher, provided emotional support and kept the books. His boss, who was also a good friend, left the door open for him to return if things didn't work out. He never had to take the offer.

Dreams aside, Monhollen became a wood carver with his eyes wide open. He planned to live on savings his first year in business in 1981. And he quit his sales job only after test marketing several wildlife carvings by showing them to galleries. Monhollen sold his works successfully through six galleries, and didn't have to live off his savings after all. But the more his works sold, the slower the payments got. "As a businessman, I won't tolerate that," he says. "And I knew I didn't have to put up with it." He won't criticize all galleries, because his experience in that market was narrow and short-lived. But he knew there had to be a better way for him.

"I was literally working seven days a week, 14 hours a day, carving as hard and as fast as I could," he says. "It became very clear to my wife and I that I would burn my body out if I continued that for very long. Plus, I wasn't using the creativity I knew I could."

That's when Monhollen put his corporate sales experience to use again. He knew most art was bought by executives and professionals—the kind of people he was used to selling to before. So he began making sales calls to market his work directly to them.

For many artists, it might be an unthinkable tactic. But not for Monhollen, who's a rare blend of businessman, artist and naturalist. He's as comfortable in a CEO's executive suite closing a deal on a wood carving as he is carving in his basement workshop or leaning over a cliff to glimpse a hawk in flight. He has the easy-going demeanor of a wood-carver who hides each day through the eight acres of forestry surrounding his Crittenden, Kentucky, home. And he has the hard-edged intensity of a salesman who doesn't mistake "no" for "never."

"I'm a carver and a marketer," he says. "I get to continue to be a businessman, but to be in control. And I get to do what I love."

He often gets leads from reading about corporate milestones or personalities in the business press. He once made an appointment with the CEO of a Fortune 500 company just because he was curious after buying some of its stock. He didn't make the sale, but he vows: "He will be a customer someday."

Getting a foot in the door isn't that hard, he says, since CEOs don't hear from too many wood-carvers who do cold calls. Once Monhollen piques their curiosity, he gives his 30-second introduction and asks for a 10-minute appointment. Usually, executives get so interested they want him to stay longer. The conversion rate is surprisingly high, he says, though he doesn't keep statistics. And even when turned down, Monhollen usually comes away with enough referrals for several more sales calls.

Once he gets a signed contract, he talks with clients to find out exactly what they want. Some have very precise ideas for their carvings. Others want suggestions, in which case Monhollen steers them toward his first love—wildlife carvings. He produces a detailed sketch for approval before committing anything to wood.

"Other than the intrinsic pleasure," he says, "the purpose of what I do is to give a company a way to say that what goes on here has to do with quality, attention to detail, and taking pride in doing the best work."

Using hand tools for almost everything but a few detailing tasks, Monhollen has carved larger-than-life pieces from such hardwoods as walnut. He also goes to great lengths to research his pieces. his biggest business expense, he says, is for travel to research his works, such as trips to Montana for two-week hikes to research some wildlife sculpts. But much of his research, and inspiration, still comes from nature closer to home.

"When I bring clients to the house, I always start by taking them for a walk in the woods," he says. "The bottom line it that this is why I'm doing what I'm doing."

CHAPTER SIX

When Someone Wants to Buy Your Work

So your neighbor wants to buy a set of Windsor chairs like the ones you just made for yourself. It's an exciting feeling to know that someone thinks enough of your work to pay for it. You probably like doing it so much that the thought of someone wanting to pay you for it never crossed your mind. But the prospect of a sale also brings a host of other questions: How much do I charge? What kind of paper do I need to make my fledgling sales efforts legal? Handling some business decisions and a little red tape are unavoidable necessities. But here are some tips for getting them done as quickly, easily and successfully as possible.

How Much Should You Charge?

Finding a fair price might seem mysterious at first. But it only involves some simple arithmetic and test sales—much simpler than some of the knotty problems you've faced trying to make joints fit. Fortunately, two methods can help you find a fair, reasonable price—formulas and the market.

You should try using a formula to price your work even if that doesn't deliver the price you finally use. Here is a simple formula to find a price that's fair. Like any pricing formula, there's a little guesswork involved in the beginning and lots of adjustment to come based on later experience. But this four-step formula is a good starting point.

Step I. Monthly Shop Expenses

Your overhead includes things you must pay for whether you sell anything or not such as utilities, equipment, maintenance, publications and membership dues to guilds and organizations.

Arriving at a figure for some of these costs involves a few calculations. For instance, you don't include the whole cost of buying a new router or table saw all at once. Instead, you use a process called depreciation. Here's how it works: Estimate the fair market value (what you think you could sell it for) of the machinery in your shop, then divide that figure by 60, which is the expected useful life of the machine with monthly equipment depreciation.

Use a similar process to figure depreciation for the shop itself. If your shop is detached from your house or was added after you bought your house, just base your figure on how much it cost to build, or the shop's fair market value (a real estate agent or appraiser can help with this). If your shop was part of your house when you bought it, you'll need to take a few more steps.

First, take the dollar value of your home and divide it by 390, which is the number of useful years for a house in the IRS depreciation tables ($32\frac{1}{2}$) times 12, to arrive at a monthly depreciation cost. Then find out the square footage of your shop; divide that number by your home's overall square footage to get the percentage of your home taken up by your shop. Multiply this number by the fraction you had before. This is part of the monthly cost of having a shop in your home.

For instance, say your 1500-square-foot home is worth $100,000. Annual depreciation ($100,000 divided by $32\frac{1}{2}$) is $3077. Monthly depreciation is $256. You use 300 square feet—or 20 percent of your home—as your shop. Depreciation on that 20 percent comes to $51 a month.

If your shop is in your garage, you'll need to do the calculation a little differently. Check with a real estate agent, or compare real estate listings in your area of similar homes with and without garages, to get an idea of how much a garage is worth. Then,

Pricing Formula

I. MONTHLY SHOP EXPENSES

1. $\div$ Equipment Value
   60 (5 years useful life)
   $\div$ ....
   ....

   = Monthly equipment overhead
   = _____

2. $\div$ Home/shop value
   390 (32½ years of useful life of
   business property)
   ....
   ....

   = Monthly shop property overhead
   = _____

3. $\times$ Monthly mortgage interest
   Fraction of home occupied by
   shop (shop square footage/total)
   ....
   ....

   = Monthly shop mortgage interest
   = _____

4. $+$ Monthly equipment overhead
   $+$ Monthly shop property overhead
   $+$ Monthly shop mortgage interest
   Other monthly shop expenses
   (utilities, materials, etc.)
   $+$ ....
   $+$ ....
   ....
   $+$ ....

   = Total monthly shop expenses
   = _____

II. HOURLY OVERHEAD

1. $\div$ Estimated hours shop used for
   paying projects
   Hours shop used for all projects
   $\div$ ....
   ....

   = Percent of hours shop used for
   paying projects
   = _____

2. $\times$ Total monthly shop expenses
   Percent of hours shop used for
   paying projects
   $\times$ ....
   ....

   = Monthly shop overhead
   = _____

3. Monthly business expenses (non-
   shop: advertising, publications,
   bookkeeping, etc.)
   $+$ Monthly shop overhead
   ....
   $+$ ....

   = Total monthly overhead
   = _____

4. $\div$ Total monthly overhead
   Hours spent on paying projects
   ....
   $\div$ ....

   = Hourly overhead
   = _____

III. HOURLY RATE

1. $\div$ Gross salary you want to make per
   year
   Hours you want to work a year
   (2000 = 40 hrs/wk + 2 wks
   vacation)
   ....
   $\div$
   ....

   = Hourly wage for you
   = _____

2. $\times$ Hourly wage for you
   10-20 percent
   ....
   ....

   = Future investment needs
   coverage
   = _____

3. $\times$ Hourly wage for you
   33 percent (or more)
   ....
   ....

   = Indirect marketing and
   administrative time coverage
   = _____

4. Hourly wage for you
   $+$ Hourly Overhead
   Future investment needs
   coverage
   $+$ Indirect marketing and
   administrative time coverage
   ....
   $+$
   $+$
   ....

   = Hourly rate
   = _____

IV. ESTIMATED PROJECT PRICE

1. $\times$ Hourly rate
   Project hours
   ....
   $\times$ ....

   = Labor and overhead
   = _____

2. Materials and other variable
   project costs
   $+$ Labor and overhead
   ....
   $+$ ....

   = Estimated project price
   = _____

figure what percentage of your garage is taken up by your shop. Divide that figure by 32½, for the years of useful life. Divide that again by 12 for a monthly depreciation figure.

For instance, if your garage is worth $5000 and your shop takes up half, that half is worth $2500. Annual depreciation comes to $77 and monthly depreciation comes to $6.

If you have a mortgage on your home, find out from your annual mortgage statement how much interest you pay. From the calculations you did earlier, find the percentage of your home's value represented by your shop. That percentage of your interest payment should also be part of your overhead calculation. If the shop isn't on separate utility meters, use the same percentage to calculate the share of monthly utility costs you should figure into overhead.

Then, add other averaged costs. Even though expenses like new saw blades will depend on how much work you do, include an average cost for these things as overhead. If you bought equipment on credit, you should also count the interest you're paying.

After you total your shop-related overhead, multiply this by the percentage of time you use your shop for projects you sell as a percentage of the overall time you spend in the shop. You get this number simply by dividing an estimate of your "business" shop hours by an estimate of your overall shop hours. If you use your shop only for projects you sell, skip this step. Otherwise, do the multiplication to come up with your total shop-related business overhead.

Then, tally up your average monthly business expenses for things not directly related to the shop, such as advertising, publications, bookkeeping, travel, etc. Adding this to shop-related expenses gives you a monthly figure.

Step II. Hourly Overhead

Now, estimate how many hours a month you spend or will spend producing work to sell. Divide the monthly overhead figure you arrived at earlier by this hourly figure. This provides an hourly overhead rate.

Step III. Your Hourly Rate

Once you finish figuring overhead, you should find this part a breeze. This is the wage you're going to pay yourself for making and selling your projects. Maybe it will be based on what you make from your job. Maybe you want less, because you enjoy woodworking so much. But don't turn yourself into a slave by paying little or nothing. The best way to determine your hourly wage is to divide the gross annual salary you want by the number of hours you want to work. For example, an annual salary of $20,000 at 40 hours per week with 2 weeks of vacation gives you an hourly wage of $10 per hour.

Besides your "wage," some other considerations need to go into your hourly rate, too. If you want to add equipment to your workshop, you need to make something extra to reinvest. You should add 10 to 20 percent to your pay rate to account for this.

And remember that besides the time you spend making something, you'll also spend time selling it and doing the recordkeeping involved in handling the sale. One way to account for this in your hourly rate is to keep records of how much time you spend selling your work and doing related paperwork in a month. Then divide that by the number of hours you spend producing it and multiply by 100. That will give you a percentage by which you can mark up your hourly rate to account for the time you spend on nonproduction work.

For instance, say you spend 30 hours a month working on projects to sell, and you spend another 10 hours selling them and doing books. Sales time equals 33 percent of your woodworking time. If your hourly pay is $15, add $5 more to account for nonproduction time. This isn't a perfect system. But it's impractical to calculate sales time for each piece. If you don't account for your sales effort, you won't be getting a fair return for your time. Now, add your hourly wage, hourly overhead, and the costs to cover reinvest and administration to form your hourly rate. This is the labor component of your price.

Step IV. Estimated Project Price

Multiply your rate by the actual number of hours you spend on a job, or an estimate of how long a project will take. Add to this all material costs, which will include any lumber, hardware, finish, etc. used on the project. This will be your project price.

What the Market Will Bear

The price you get from the formula may not be what customers are willing to pay. It may be higher or lower. You can find out how well the market will accept your prices in a couple of ways. One is checking out what others are charging for similar work at fairs or stores. Another is plunging in and setting up a booth or approaching retailers and gauging the reactions. If things sell quickly, you may be safe in raising your prices. If your work doesn't sell at all, or retailers tell you they can't get the prices you're asking, it's time to rethink. Your options include:

- Lowering your expenses by using different materials or cutting overhead.
- Finding ways to make the product more quickly—thus maintaining your hourly rate.
- Scrapping the product and trying to sell something else.
- Lowering your hourly pay.
- Trying some new sales outlets.

The last option shouldn't be overlooked. Don't base your decision on the results of one or two shows or comments from one or two stores. Try more upscale stores or shows first. Maybe the products and price were right, but the places were wrong. Pricing is an intricate craft; ultimately, trial and error will help you develop prices that work best for you.

Keeping Records

It is easier to make money than to keep track of it. And it can be tempting to ignore the recordkeeping entirely for a hobby-business. But that's a dangerous approach. Even if you don't keep records for yourself, you'll need them for Uncle Sam. To ignore the records is to risk paying much more than you should in taxes or risk an audit and a stiff penalty. Here are some simple tools to keep your records straight and keep you out of hot water.

- *Receipts.* Get and keep them for everything you spend on your woodworking. Later on, you can sort out the ones that aren't related to work you sell. Even if you don't keep a timely record of your expenses, do keep your receipts in some kind of order according to expense category, such as materials, travel, advertising, etc. A simple set of envelopes for each category will do the trick. Keeping all your receipts lumped together in a shoe box is better than not keeping them at all. But it will make your job much harder at tax time, or your tax preparation costs much higher.
- *Invoices.* You should prepare simple invoices for sales to stores, since they'll want documentation for their own records. Though many artisans don't provide them, issuing cash receipts at craft shows also can help you track your income and keep your name in front of customers.
- *Ledger or Bookkeeping System.* Your sales and

Lasting Impressions
3033 Sawdust Lane
Red Oak, Iowa 51566
(712) 555-0023

INVOICE

TO: Mary Smith
Enchanted Forest Crafts
13 Folklore Lane
Lorelei, CT 02155

Invoice No.	2033
Purchase Order No.	1504

Date:	March 4, 1993
Due Date:	April 3, 1993

Date Shipped	Date Ordered	Item Purchased	Quantity	Unit Price	Total
3/4/93	2/4/93	Miniature chair	4	$25.00	$100.00
3/4/93	2/4/93	Miniature table	1	$100.00	$100.00

Total (Please pay this amount):	$200.00

Terms: Payment is due within 30 days of invoice date. Past due balances subject to finance charge of 1.5% per month.

Thank you for your prompt remittance!

Here are the basics needed in any invoice. Consignment deals work differently, but you may still send an invoice to help document your shipment and spell out the terms of your arrangement. Terms are obviously different than an outright sale. But you may still want to specify such terms with a statement like: "Payment is due upon sale. A finance charge of 1.5% per month will be charged on balances more than 30 days past due." The finance charge may not be legally enforceable, but it does get across the message that you expect prompt payment.

record-keeping duties should be simple enough to let you keep your own record of income and expenses. Even if you have no experience in bookkeeping or accounting, a simple, ready-made bookkeeping system can help. You may ask an accountant to help you set up a simple ledger system—which won't cost much. An even cheaper alternative is buying a *Dome Simplified Weekly Bookkeeping Record*, which is an easy-to-use single-entry bookkeeping system available in any office supply store. The Dome book provides clear explanation of how to keep your expense categories straight. And it provides room for a journal of the money you bring in and pay out.

- *Mileage and Travel Expense Log.* If you do any traveling at all for your business, you can write

off expenses. Mileage for trips to the lumberyard, craft show or sales calls can all be deducted at the current mileage rate issued each year by the Internal Revenue Service. But you must keep a timely record of your business trips. For each trip, record the date, beginning mileage on your odometer, ending mileage, where you went and the business purpose of the trip. Logs available in business supply stores will do the job. So will a log you make yourself, provided it contains complete information. If you travel to craft shows, transportation, lodging and meal expenses will be deductible against your income. But you must keep your receipts and a log of these expenses. Records of dates, places and business reasons are required for each expense.

Again, your own customized journal or a log available from a business supply store will do the job.

Do You Need Help With Your Bookkeeping?

If you don't trust yourself to do the job—and your spouse isn't willing, able or interested—you may want to turn to an outside bookkeeping service. Keeping your records on computer is another possibility. The growing array of personal finance software includes plenty of options that can help you track business finances, too. Some check-writing programs can help you write checks, enter expenses and balance your checkbook at the same time. Buying a computer simply for record keeping, however, probably isn't a good idea. Your bookkeeping needs really aren't that extensive. For the $2,000 or so you'd spend on a computer system, you can buy a lot of bookkeeping help.

Whether you get help with bookkeeping or not, you probably will need help with tax preparation. Your tax return may deal with complicated issues, like accelerated depreciation, inventory accounting and cost of goods sold. At least for the first year you sell your work, it would be wise to consult an accountant or an enrolled agent (a specially trained tax preparer, frequently a former IRS employee).

What Else Do I Need to Be Legal?

Besides paying income taxes on your woodworking income, you may need to tackle a few other legal and administrative chores. Rules vary widely from state to state. Fortunately, your task is easier if you don't hire employees. Here are some areas to consider:

- *Business licenses.* You may need to get a vendor's license or business license from your county or local government. Look under "Vendor's Licenses" or "Business Licenses" in the government listings of the phone book for a number to call near you. You may not need a license, so ask what the requirements are before dropping in. Some localities may not require licenses for businesses that take in money only occasionally and in small amounts. But most do require some kind of business license if you sell anything at all. And it's not that difficult or expensive to keep your operation legal. Increasingly, local and state governments are making the process easier for new business ventures through "one-stop" centers. So you may be able to take care of any other necessary documentation or registrations when you get your vendor's license. If not, your local chamber of commerce also may provide information on what's needed.

- *Sales taxes.* Most states and some cities may levy sales taxes on the items you sell. If you sell a service, like refinishing, you're less likely to have to pay this tax. Getting a vendor's license generally sets you up for paying sales taxes, too. You should receive information on when and where to remit taxes when you get the license. In practice, a lot of craft sales are in the untaxed "underground" segment of the economy. But some states, such as New York, have targeted craft show and other fair exhibitors for special enforcement actions in recent years. As states struggle for new ways to raise revenue, you can expect more of this. So skirting your duties to pay sales taxes can get you in trouble. Craft show organizers should provide the necessary forms and information about taxes in their area.

What's Zoning, and How Does It Apply to You?

Zoning—the set of land-use laws enacted by most localities—can be the bane of home woodworkers. Homes generally are in a residential zone. Factories are in an industrial zone. Shops and offices are in a commercial zone. Except for specially planned developments, localities like to keep things that way. So zoning codes usually won't let you operate a woodworking business in a residential or commercial zone. You can do your woodworking as a hobby all you want. But when you start taking money for it, it may be considered a business. If you can demonstrate that your woodworking is simply a hobby and any income is incidental, you should still have no problem.

Zoning laws can't be used to close businesses that were operating on land before they went into effect. So, if you were operating a woodworking business on your property before the zoning code took effect, and you can prove it, you should be protected. But such a "grandfather clause" usually won't apply if you buy the property from someone else who was operating a manufacturing business there.

Fortunately, with zoning, there's usually no crime if there's no victim. If your neighbors don't mind your woodworking, or don't know you're doing it for money, the authorities won't likely get involved. But if a neighbor complains, you could have a problem. So, unless you're surrounded by lots of land or other noise buffers, do whatever you can to keep your woodworking from being a nuisance to neighbors.

CHAPTER •Checklist

DETERMINE HOW MUCH YOU SHOULD CHARGE
- ☐ Figure monthly shop expenses
- ☐ Figure hourly overhead
- ☐ Figure your houly rate
- ☐ Estimate the project's price

KEEP GOOD RECORDS
- ☐ Keep all your receipts
- ☐ Use invoices for sales
- ☐ Keep a ledger or a bookkeeping system
- ☐ Keep a mileage and travel expense log

ADDRESS LEGAL CONSIDERATIONS
- ☐ Business licenses
- ☐ Sales taxes
- ☐ Zoning laws

What to Do if Your Hobby Is Turning Into a Business

It could be the best or worst thing to happen to a woodworker. But once you start selling your work, sooner or later you may face the choice of turning it into a full-time, full-fledged business. The choice may come because what used to be a hobby takes up so much time it's become a second job. Or it may be that you've been laid off or prospects in your career are looking bleak. Ideally, the choice comes because you're making so much money so painlessly that you might as well quit your day job.

When faced with this choice, it's important to think about why you started woodworking, and selling your work, in the first place. If your goal was to escape all the hassles of the business world, maybe plunging into woodworking as a business isn't for you. But running a woodworking business doesn't have to be a hassle. The nice thing is that you're the boss. You can decide how much growth you really want and the type of work you want to do.

Is Your Hobby Becoming a Business?

The important thing is to recognize the signs of a hobby on the brink of becoming a business. Then, you can make a decision that could save you considerable stress and confusion later. Here are a few signs of when your hobby is becoming a business.

- Your woodworking income not only supports your hobby, but also makes you a tidy profit.
- Paperwork and planning take up an increasing share of your time.
- What you make is dictated more by what customers want than by what you enjoy making.

- You spend increasing time on woodworking and less time on other interests, even when you'd rather be doing something else.
- You have to reschedule family activities, work or sleep to get out an order.

Once you've found your woodworking is turning into a business, it's time to consider if that's really the direction you want to take. Here are some factors to consider:

- Do you have the self-discipline to be your own boss?
- Are your long-term career prospects as a woodworker better than in your current job, including such tangible factors as wages and benefits and intangibles such as personal satisfaction?
- Can you afford the risk, especially if you need to borrow to set up a full-time shop?
- Can your home workshop accommodate the inventory, tools and work load necessary for a full-time business?
- Do you have enough savings or solid orders to get you through the start-up period? Most financial planners recommend you have enough cash or credit available to cover at least two months of living expenses. Even if you have orders to start out, you may have to wait thirty days or more after completion of the orders to receive payment.
- How will you provide for health insurance? Do you have a working spouse whose plan will cover you? If not, can you arrange other coverage affordably?
- Will your homeowner's policy cover insurance of a business you run in your home?
- What are the zoning implications of running a business from your home?
- If you can't run the business from your home,

can you afford the cost of buying or renting a workshop and office elsewhere?

Expanding Your Income Without Expanding Your Work Load

Deciding against going into business full-time doesn't mean your enterprise has to stop growing. You can expand income, even from a hobby, by working smarter instead of harder. Some time-tested methods are:

- *Charge more for your work.* Don't let your modesty make your life difficult. Many talented woodworkers, especially hobbyists, charge too little for their work. The more experience you develop, and the better reputation you build, the more people are willing to pay for your work. You may lose some customers when you charge more. But unless your goal is continuing expansion of sales, that's probably not a problem. Even if your overall sales slip, what you bring in per hour will increase. Price is an important tool for regulating your work load and getting enough money to make your time worthwhile.

- *Move into more lucrative niches.* Depending on your flexibility, you may be able to increase your income per hour merely by moving into new types of crafts. Turning artistic one-of-a-kind bowls, for instance, is one area that seems to offer the best return for talented turners. In general, items that are original creations or are more decorative than functional seem to offer better returns than more functional items. Refinishing or restoration work, while readily available, tends to offer lower returns than creating original reproductions.

- *Improve productivity.* Jigs and other shortcuts can make any job move faster. But you won't have to cut the price. The result is more profit per piece. Many of these shortcuts you'll learn yourself as you work. But joining local woodworking groups, buying books and subscribing to woodworking publications are great ways to learn from the experiences of other woodworkers. The time and money you invest will more than pay for themselves.

Getting Someone Else to Back You

Even if you've been woodworking for years, going into a full-time business can take a substantial investment. You may need to buy more tools to upgrade for a bigger work load. Or you may just need a line of credit to tide you over while you establish markets.

If possible, it's best to rely on your own funds. Starting a business is always hard. Starting it in debt is harder. Unless you have an urgent need to start a full-fledged business—perhaps because you lost your job—you should use your sideline business to generate a cash reserve first. If you absolutely must rely on other people's money, however, here are some sources.

- *Banks.* A small business with no track record can expect a hard time getting a loan. But you have a better chance with a bank where you have a long-standing relationship, such as checking accounts, mortgage and car loans, etc. If nothing

Keeping the Fun Along With the Profit

For Joseph Ferola, wood turning is still a hobby. The only difference is, his natural-edge bowls sell for up to $800 a piece, and he's sold about 800 of them since 1987. He didn't really need the money after retiring as an engineer with a pension from the Connecticut Department of Transportation. But the Windsor, Connecticut, turner doesn't believe the money spoils his fun any, either.

"I've always been interested in wood, and I knew when I retired I'd be doing something in wood, either furniture or something else," Ferola says. "My brother had a cheap lathe he'd bought to do some special work. And then a friend of his gave him a larger lathe, and he gave me the smaller one."

Ferola started spindle turning in 1986, but soon tried his hand at turning bowls. He built his skills through practice and attending every local workshop he could find. Within six months, he decided to try his hand at selling some work. He had made a bowl from a beautifully figured piece of ash hardwood and submitted a slide to the juried "Vessels and Forms" show at the May 1987 Houston Festival in Texas. He was surprised when jurors accepted his bowl, and shocked when someone actually bought it for $380. "I said, 'My God, this is a lot of fun.' Once you get lucky like that, you figure there may be something to this."

Since then, his work has been displayed at dozens of museums from California to Massachusetts and featured in *Bon Appetit* and *Yankee* magazines. Commercial success has let Ferola trade up to a $2000 lathe that holds blocks or burls up to two-feet wide, a breathing helmet and professional-strength dust collection system. But even though he turns pieces almost every day, he does it for fun. And he prefers to do most of his sales through galleries so he doesn't have to fuss with sending slides to juries or tending to booths at shows. Overhead certainly doesn't force Ferola to keep selling his work. His equipment is virtually his only cost, since most of his pieces are made from found wood.

"It's a beautiful thing to do in retirement," he says. "I'm doing what I enjoy. It's always nice to have people pay money for your stuff, and you can always use the income. But I still have my retirement income, so I'm not dependent on selling these things. I can relax or go on vacation if I want to. If I don't feel like doing anything some days, I just don't do it."

Joseph Ferola considers turning wood bowls like this a hobby. But it's a hobby that now provides sales of several hundred dollars for some pieces and a comfortable supplement to his retirement income. The difference between this "business" and a job is that Ferola can stop working and do something else any time he wants.

else, they have to worry about losing your business if they turn you down. You may be able to get a line of credit by using your equipment, workshop or accounts receivable as collateral.

Some banks offer microloan programs for businesses that need only $500 to $5000 in seed capital to get going. Many of these programs are specifically geared to women and minority businesses or to people currently on public assistance.

If you have substantial equity in your home, it may be easier just to take out a second mortgage. This way, you won't have to provide the bank with a business plan or information about your business. And the interest is fully tax-deductible. This approach only works, however, if, in the eyes of the bank, you still have a job that brings in enough income to allow you to pay back the loan.

- *Credit cards.* You may also tap existing bank credit cards as your "line of credit." But this is by far the costliest route because of the steep interest. It's only advisable if you're sure you can pay off the balance within a few months of tapping it.

- *Small Business Administration.* Small businesses that can prove they've been turned down by conventional lenders may seek loans guaranteed by the U.S. Small Business Administration, a branch of the Department of Commerce.

   Such loans, however, require considerable paperwork and time. If you go this route, your local chamber of commerce can be valuable in helping you find your way. Some local governments and chambers also back small-business loans, often in cooperation with the SBA.

- *Customers.* Your relationship with a key customer or customers may be such that they would be willing to provide financing for your fledgling business. This is particularly true if you're a key supplier to a well-heeled store or interior design firm. Financing could take the form of an outright loan or an advance on future orders. Obviously, you must have a very close working relationship before you can suggest such a deal. And keep in mind that the risk this customer takes will be repaid, with interest, through your everlasting loyalty and reliability, in addition to the goods or money.

- *Family.* Here, as in other areas of life, the Bank of Mom and Dad may be open for business. This is the best place to find a lender who won't repossess your home or break your arm if you miss payments. But the strain on the relationship may be just as damaging.

Insurance Needs

Going into business for yourself means assuming many new risks. The more insurance you can afford to hedge against these risks, the better you'll sleep at night. Insurance won't guarantee success. But it can prevent you from being wiped out by unforeseen calamities.

Your home owner's insurance policy may not cover equipment and materials you use for a business in your home. Even if it does, chances are that running a woodworking business, and the attendant fire risks, will increase your premiums. Also, a home owner's policy won't pay for the business you lose as a result of a fire or other calamity. For that, you'll need business continuation coverage as part of a business policy.

You may be able to get protection from lawsuits connected with your business through a liability umbrella offered as part of your home owner's policy. But make sure such an umbrella will cover all possible suits against you, including product liability.

If you believe the chance of a suit is small, you may just want to "go bare," or shoulder the risk without insurance. Keep in mind, however, that unless you take the complicated and sometimes costly step of incorporating your business, you could lose your home and other personal property in a legal judgment. As a practical matter, many professional woodworkers find business, property, casualty and liability insurance can be prohibitively expensive or even impossible to get. Unfortunately, there's no easy solution to this problem, other than shopping around and managing your risks as well as possible, possibly through incorporating your business. A good business insurance agent can help you find the best deal available and provide tips on any changes you can make to lower your insurance costs.

If you hire employees, you'll need a worker's compensation insurance policy to cover any on-the-job injuries they may suffer. Many states provide worker's compensation coverage. If not, you'll need to arrange coverage through a business insurance agent. Even states that don't run their own worker's compensation system may require employers to purchase private insurance.

You'll also have to pay unemployment insurance to your state, premiums for which will vary depending on how many claims are filed against your business by employees.

Health insurance is likely to be the most expensive burden you'll take on with a new business, even if you have no employees. You can get coverage for up to 18 months from your former employer's plan under the federal COBRA law. But you'll have to pay 102 percent of the employer's premium. After that, you're on your own.

Unless you can arrange family coverage with a spouse, you'll have to seek an individual policy or group coverage through a membership organization. Generally, either of these options will mean less coverage, higher premiums or both compared to coverage through an employer.

A number of membership groups offer health coverage as one of their benefits. But beware of some groups targeted to small businesses or the self-employed. They may really operate as fronts for insurance companies and offer hospitalization plans with scant coverage for nonhospital expenses. With any plan, find out exactly what kind of costs are excluded from coverage, if and when your coverage can be cancelled and how preexisting medical conditions and maternity care are covered.

Woodworkers may be better served by group coverage through their local chamber of commerce or through such groups as the American Craft Association. Some local organizations such as the Michigan Guild of Artists and Artisans, Pennsylvania Guild of Craftsmen, Tennessee Association of Craft Artists and Ohio Designer Craftsmen also offer group medical insurance for members.

From Hobby to Business

David T. Smith was a diesel mechanic before he became a full-time cabinet-maker in 1980. Today, he runs The Workshops of David T. Smith, a Morrow, Ohio, wholesale and retail furniture, pottery and antique-reproduction business that grosses more than $2 million annually. His pieces have been bought by Jacqueline Onassis, Connie Chung and designer Ralph Lauren. But he started as a hobbyist, whose love and study of American antiques was and is the basis of his work.

David Smith demonstrates how leaves for one of the antique-reproduction tables on display fit together. Smith's love of antiques and woodworking have turned into a $2-million-a-year business. Love of woodworking made the production side of business a pleasure for David Smith. But his lack of business background made The Workshops of David T. Smith less profitable than it could have been.

"I'm first of all a student of this stuff," Smith says. "A lot of other people are in it for the buck. The people I have working for me are very interested in it, too. You have to make a living at it, but that's almost secondary. The first thing is that we enjoy what we're doing and have a real interest in the history."

Like most woodworkers, Smith started by building pieces for his own home. From there, he branched into doing restoration and repair work for antiques he acquired for himself, then for other people. Eventually, he decided his sideline could become a full-time job.

"Times were hard at first," he says. But he soon heard about a job at the nearby Kings Island amusement park—an order for 200 tables and 400 benches. It was mass production work, unlike the one-of-a-kind antique reproductions that were his specialty. But he needed the business, so he submitted a bid. It was by far the lowest, he says. And though he barely made a profit on the job, it was a turning point that got Smith's woodworking business going full-speed.

"I really had no idea what I was doing," he admits now. "One minute I was making antique reproductions. The next minute I'm doing 200 tables and 400 benches." Fortunately, he had plenty of land and a workshop that could handle the job. With the huge order in hand, he hired employees.

After the job was done, Smith had to decide what to do next with the employees and the equipment he had accumulated. He decided to develop a line of reproduction furniture that he sold to antique dealers and a few retailers he knew. Smith also began developing the museum-quality finish which became his hallmark, and working with elaborately figured boards. He developed a network of retail customers throughout the East and Midwest, and a reputation for high-end reproductions priced as high as $4000.

It's been years now since he's actually built a piece himself, but Smith still spends time hunting for premium quality boards around the country and finishing pieces built by others in his shop. And he manages the business—a role that took the biggest adjustment.

"I have no business education or college degree," he says, though he believes he

As Smith has concentrated on learning more about business, a computer has helped him get a better grasp on costs and pricing.

always had the savvy needed to run a business. "Still, it's hard to go from being a cabinetmaker and finisher and getting your hands dirty to going in and working on a computer to do taxes and payroll or cash flow analysis. It takes time to adapt." He's grown to take as much pride in building a business as in building furniture.

Smith bought a personal computer in 1989, which he used to begin formally analyzing the costs of pieces for the first time. To his amazement, he found the shop was making widely varying profits on similarly priced pieces. So he began working on slowing growth of the business and concentrating on improving profitability. And he still wants to maintain the best qualities of a one-man shop, trying when he can to have only one or two cabinetmakers work on each piece rather than dividing the work up assembly-line style.

"What's unique for a business this size is that we're still a bench shop," he says. "We've developed a wholesale line. But when someone comes off the street with an antique magazine and wants a highboy done in curly maple with carving on the shelves just so, we can do that, too."

CHAPTER
•Checklist

DETERMINE IF YOUR HOBBY IS BECOMING A BUSINESS

☐ Income supports your hobby and makes a tidy profit

☐ Paperwork and planning take up more of your time

☐ Consumer demand dictates what you make

☐ Woodworking takes up more than your "hobby time"

CONSIDER THESE FACTORS BEFORE STARTING A BUSINESS

☐ Can you be your own boss?

☐ Will a new business be better than your current job?

☐ Can you afford the risk to set up shop?

☐ Can your workshop accommodate a full-time business?

☐ Can you afford the start up period?

☐ How will you provide for health insurance?

☐ What zoning laws do you have to consider?

☐ Can you afford to buy or rent a workshop and office?

EXPAND YOUR INCOME WITHOUT INCREASING YOUR WORK

☐ Charge more for your work

☐ Move into more lucrative niches

☐ Improve productivity

GETTING SOMEONE ELSE TO BACK YOU

☐ Banks

☐ Credit cards

☐ Small Business Administration

☐ Customers

☐ Family

CHAPTER EIGHT

Money Management

Keeping as much as you can of what you earn is just as important as building a good product and selling it for a fair price. Even great woodworkers can make mistakes managing the money side of things. When that happens, it can mean lots of hard work going to scrap. This chapter is aimed at helping you make the most of the money your woodworking earns.

Taxing Issues for Hobbyists

The government will want a piece of any money you make from woodworking. If you bring in more money selling a piece of furniture than you spent building it, you've got income that must be reported to the IRS. Like other hobbyists, many woodworkers probably don't report that income. Failing to report such earnings, however, is not only illegal, but risky. If you deposit income from woodworking sales in your bank account, you've created a money trail that the IRS may follow in an audit. Besides, doing things on the up-and-up doesn't have to cost you that much in taxes if you plan it right.

Whether you make money from your woodworking or not, the IRS may still consider you a hobbyist. That can have important, though not always bad, implications for your income taxes. Generally, the IRS considers an enterprise a business if it turns a profit for three of five consecutive years. But that yardstick doesn't help you much in your first year. Nor is it the only factor the IRS uses in separating hobbyists from business operators. Other factors the IRS considers are:

- Whether your woodworking is principally for your enjoyment rather than to make money. (If

you intend to treat your woodworking income as business income, don't go around saying things like, "I just do this for the love of working with wood, not to make money.")

- Whether you operate in a businesslike manner, for instance, by keeping complete and accurate financial records.
- How much time you spend on woodworking and selling your work. The more time, the more likely you'll be considered engaged in a woodworking business.
- Whether you've been a professional woodworker or woodworking employee in the past.
- Whether woodworking is your sole source of income.

If you're a hobbyist, you must still report any money you make from selling your work as income. But if you don't itemize deductions on your tax form, you can't deduct any woodworking expenses as a hobbyist. Even if you do itemize, you may only deduct the amount of woodworking expenses that, combined with a handful of other deductible expenses, exceeds 2 percent of your taxable income from all sources. And you can't deduct woodworking expenses not directly attributable to the pieces you sell. In other words, you can't deduct seminars you take or subscriptions you buy unless they were solely for projects you sold. And to deduct equipment expenses, you would have to keep a log showing how much time you spent using the equipment for pieces you sold versus pieces you made for yourself or for pleasure. Finally, you can't deduct more in hobby expenses than you made in hobby income. For these reasons, some people would rather be considered a business.

But being a hobbyist isn't all bad—even from a tax standpoint. For one thing, the tax form will be easier.

You still need to keep records of your income and expenses. But you only have to report income on one line, expenses on another. Filing as a business means using two new forms—Schedule C and Schedule SE—plus more in some cases. Sure, hobbyists have to pay income tax on what they make. But they don't have to pay self-employment tax on it. Self-employment tax is an additional tax bite of about 13 percent of income that covers Social Security and Medicare taxes for the self-employed. If you have a self-employment income of more than $400, you must pay self-employment tax even on income from a sideline like woodworking. So, when you consider all these factors, it might be to your advantage to pay taxes as a hobbyist instead of as a business.

One key factor here is how much you're already making apart from woodworking. If your income is over $60,000 or so, you've already maxed out on most Social Security and Medicare taxes. So any income from woodworking would be subject to little if any self-employment tax. In that case, being considered a "business" by the IRS probably would be to your advantage. If you make less than $60,000, however, being a hobbyist may work better.

Here are some hypothetical examples. Joe is a carpenter who makes $25,000 a year and has a mortgage that lets him itemize deductions. He makes another $3000 from selling furniture, with expenses of only $1000. If the IRS considers him a hobbyist, he'd pay $375 on the money he made from woodworking. But if Joe's woodworking were considered a business, he'd pay $562. On the other hand, consider Gary, who's a lawyer making $85,000 a year. He, too, makes an extra $3000 selling furniture he made, less only $1000 in expenses. He can't deduct any of his hobby expenses because they total less than 2 percent of his overall income. Gary would pay $840 in taxes on

his woodworking profit if taxed as a hobbyist, but only $618 if taxed as a business.

What works best for you depends on many individual factors. The best idea is to get a copy of a current tax form or last year's tax return and work out what you would owe as a hobbyist compared to a business. Then, you can try to tailor your approach so you'll qualify for the best treatment. Don't get carried away, though. The amount you'll save on taxes probably won't justify hours of worrying or making big changes in how you operate.

When Being a Business Can Be Good

Hobbyists and businesses alike may deduct a variety of woodworking expenses from their woodworking income. Any ordinary and necessary cost of running a woodworking business is fair game for deduction. That includes any supplies, shipping costs, selling costs, travel expenses to craft shows, and other mileage, such as to the lumberyard. For hobbyists, however, the expenses must be for the projects you sold, not the ones you made for yourself or gave away.

If you qualify as a business, your ability to deduct expenses expands greatly. So, even if your woodworking is no more than a sideline, it may pay to handle your taxes like a business. In some cases, you might be able to deduct the entire price of a new power tool the year you buy it. You may even be able to deduct losses from your woodworking against your other income from the present or future. These net operating losses (NOLs) could be quite valuable.

But keep in mind that you can't just decide to file your taxes as a business because it's convenient or profitable to do so. You have to really be operating a business in the eyes of the IRS, using the criteria described earlier. The feds are very sensitive to hobbies being passed off as businesses merely to create tax deductions. So forget NOLs, unless you already have three years of woodworking profit under your belt in the past five years, or you can otherwise make a very compelling case that your woodworking operation is a business.

Here are some other conditions that apply if you want to deduct losses from your woodworking business against other income.

- You can't use expenses of a home workshop or office to create a loss that's deducted against other income. (You can, however, deduct home shop/office expenses up to where you break even, and carry over any additional loss to future years.)

- You can't deduct more in losses than you actually have at risk, such as your investment in woodworking equipment, supplies, etc.

- You can't deduct the full cost of a new piece of woodworking equipment if that deduction creates a loss for your woodworking venture.

Home-Shop/Office Deduction

If you run what qualifies as a woodworking business from your home, you may be able to deduct costs for the mortgage interest, insurance, utilities, and maintenance and upkeep of that part of your home where you run the operation. You may even be able to write off some of your home's value against your taxable income. The deduction is proportional to the percentage of space in your home devoted to your workshop, storage of inventory and supplies, and any office space you use to handle paperwork. But as you should expect by now with the IRS, you'll have to jump through some hoops first.

- You'll have to fill out another form—Form 8829.

- The area you deduct must be used regularly and exclusively for business, or for inventory storage. And you must be able to document this.

- You need to do the measurements to determine the business percentage of your home. And you can't just take that percentage of your home's value. First, you must subtract the value of the land your home sits on from its overall value. To get that figure, you may need to contact your local tax office or get an appraisal.

The paperwork hassles alone are enough to scare many people away from taking this deduction. Plus, many think the home-office (or shop) deduction is a red flag that increases chances for an audit. But at least estimate how much the deduction could be worth to you. If it's legitimate, don't be scared away from taking it.

Equipment Deductions

Most woodworking equipment can be "depreciated" over five years for tax purposes if used in a business. That basically means taking the purchase price of the equipment, dividing it by five, and deducting that number from the income your woodworking produces for five years. Usually, you can only do this if you qualify as a business, since the IRS will say you bought the equipment for pleasure if you're a hobbyist. As a hobbyist, you might be able to deduct the cost of a piece of equipment if you could prove it was purchased solely for money-making projects. Or, you could deduct part of the cost for the percentage of time you used the tool on money-making projects. But the time needed to document that probably wouldn't justify the effort.

As a business, you can take advantage of Section 179, which lets woodworkers or other businesses deduct the full price of up to $17,500 in new equipment the year it's purchased. That gives you the tax deduction right away rather than in five annual installments. Buying equipment under Section 179 can be an especially good way to eat up any extra income in December so you won't have to pay taxes on it in April. Section 179 is one of the tax code's nicest breaks for the little guy. Bigger businesses can't use it because the deduction is phased out for businesses that invest $200,000 a year or more in new equipment. Some states also offer tax credits to qualified businesses that invest in equipment. Check with your accountant or the state tax, development or commerce department for details.

You can't use a Section 179 deduction to create a loss, but you can use it to the point you break even, then carry the rest of the deduction over to future years. Normally, you may only deduct one-quarter of the year's depreciation for equipment you buy in December on that year's tax return. That would mean you could only deduct 5 percent the first year and the remaining 95 percent over the following four years. So Section 179 can be a very valuable tool for getting the most tax benefit from a purchase.

Other year-end tax-saving ideas include:

- Not billing customers for any orders until late enough in December that you don't actually get the cash until January.
- Loading up on tax-deductible supplies you'll need for the coming year in December.
- Using earnings from your woodworking to set up a Keogh plan or SEP-IRA for retirement. You can qualify for either even if you don't qualify for a regular IRA deduction. Banks, insurance companies and mutual fund companies all can provide details on each type of option.

Can You Deduct the Cost of Becoming a Better Woodworker?

Honing your skills through classes, seminars or publications can definitely improve your enjoyment of the hobby. It may also generate tax deductions. That shouldn't be a factor in whether you decide to buy a book or take a class. But you should take the deduction if you deserve it.

For people considered hobbyists by the IRS, taking such deductions can be difficult. The only way you could deduct the cost of a book, magazine, course, etc., would be if you could prove you took it solely to help you produce a particular moneymaking project or group of such projects. If the IRS considers you a business, however, your deduction horizons broaden considerably. Most of the costs of bettering your woodworking skills will be fully deductible. Examples of skill-improvement tax deductions are:

- *Costs of magazine subscriptions, books, videos and membership dues you spend to better your skills.* These all would be listed separately as miscellaneous expenses on Schedule C. Be sure to break out your miscellaneous expenses into as many reasonable categories as you can. A big lump-sum "miscellaneous" line looks suspicious to the IRS.
- *Expenses for classes or seminars you take may be deductible.* The rules here are more complicated. If the class you take is an "ordinary and necessary" cost of doing your woodworking, it should be deductible as a miscellaneous expense on Schedule C. Educational expenses are also deductible as employee expenses on Schedule A. But unless you're already an employee of a woodworking shop, you probably can't take the deduction here. Generally, you must already be a woodworker to deduct the cost of woodworking classes. A course is not deductible if it's not related somehow to your job or sideline business, if it's needed to meet the minimum educational requirements of a job or sideline business, or if it qualifies you for a new trade or profession.
- *The cost of traveling to classes may also be deductible.* Keep in mind, a trip to the Smokies to

Tax Preparation: Do You Need Professional Advice?

If you plan to file taxes as a business, by all means seek professional advice from an accountant, enrolled agent or lawyer. Storefront tax-preparation companies often don't understand enough about your kind of business to be of much help. The forms and the rules are so much more complicated than even a personal tax form that you need either special training or special help to deal with them. At the very least, get professional help the first year you report woodworking income as a business. That way, you'll get set up properly to handle the work yourself in future years.

Hobbyists with fairly small and easy-to-track operations probably can handle the work themselves. But if you have a lot of questions about what should or shouldn't count as income, what you may deduct, or whether you qualify as a business or hobbyist, seek professional guidance.

take a class has to actually be a business trip. You can have some fun while you're there. But you can't take a two-day course during a two-week trip and expect to deduct all the expenses as a business trip.

Unlike home-office expenses and Section 179 equipment expenses, the costs of improving your skills can be used to create a loss for your woodworking sideline business. Reason, of course, is the key. If you cleared $2000 selling your projects and then spent $5000 traveling to and taking woodworking classes, the IRS will smell something rotten.

Planning for Tax Time

The money you make selling your woodworking projects may come as a pleasant surprise. But the taxes you owe on that money can come as a shock in April.

That's one reason it's important to put some of your woodworking earnings aside to take care of Uncle Sam and all his hungry cousins in state and local government. Also, federal, state and local tax laws call for you to estimate and pay the income tax you owe on a quarterly basis. If you wait until April to pay all the taxes, you may owe penalties on top of the taxes.

You'll need to fill out IRS Form 1040-ES to arrive at a figure for estimated quarterly tax payments. State and local governments have equivalent forms. You can obtain all the forms you need at the main branch of your public library or by calling the IRS and state or local tax departments. Generally, you won't have to pay penalties if you pay at least as much in withholding and estimated taxes for the current tax year as the total amount of tax you paid the previous year.

But avoiding penalties doesn't always mean you avoid a big, unexpected tax bill. That's why keeping simple books to record income and expenses on a weekly or monthly basis is important. If you don't know how much you're making, you won't know how much to put aside.

This record keeping doesn't have to be complicated. You can just keep a log that tallies the difference between what you make and your related expenses. This is your net income from woodworking. You can always work on separating the expenses into the appropriate categories later. The most important thing is to have some idea of how much you're earning.

One rule of thumb is to put aside a third to a half of your net earnings from woodworking sales to pay taxes (a third if you fall into the 15 percent federal income tax bracket, half if you fall into the 28 percent bracket or higher). You can draw on this fund to pay your estimated income taxes. And you'll probably still have a little left over at the end of the year, which you can use to splurge.

Other Taxes

Besides tax on woodworking income you make, you may also be required to pay property taxes on woodworking equipment used for business purposes. Most states exempt up to $100,000 of equipment from such taxes, but you may still need to file a form for the state's accounting purposes. You may also be required to pay taxes on your inventory of finished products or materials. Your state department of taxation or county auditor can provide forms, or you may be registered to receive forms when you get your business license.

On the plus side, if your woodworking qualifies as a business, you may be able to get an exemption on sales taxes for any production equipment you buy. Rules to qualify and get such exemptions are complicated and vary from state to state. You can check with an accountant, your local chamber of commerce, or the state's taxation department for details.

Develop a Plan

Beyond tax planning, woodworkers need basic business planning. That's true whether it's a hobby or a full-fledged business. A plan can help you make more money with less effort. If you started building a chest of drawers without a plan, you'd probably end up wasting lots of wood and time. Selling your work without a plan can be just as wasteful. Having a plan doesn't by any means guarantee things will turn out the way you expect, just as having a set of project plans doesn't guarantee the project will turn out right. But a plan does increase the odds that any surprises will be pleasant ones.

Most pieces that should go into your plan have already been covered in this book. Your plan ties those elements together into a blueprint you can use to guide your efforts. Here are the questions your plan should answer.

- What is your specialty? And what makes your work different and better than what's generally available or otherwise desirable?
- Who will buy what you make? Think of the types of people, where they live, shop, etc.
- How do you get to those customers (craft fairs, stores, etc.) considering both what you make and the kinds of selling settings in which you're comfortable?
- What kinds of promotional and sales tools do you need to get people to notice your work?
- What are your space and equipment needs?
- How much will it cost to make your product, and how much should you charge to compensate yourself reasonably for your time?
- How much money do you need to invest to get started making the product, put together promotional material, etc.?
- Can you start out small, making and selling one or a few pieces before getting in deeper and investing a lot of time and money?
- How much money do you want to make? Just enough to pay for more equipment and supplies to make your hobby more enjoyable? Or do you want more, either as a supplemental source of income or, possibly, a new career?
- What licenses or other paperwork do you need to meet legal requirements?

Where You Can Get Free Help

Your local chamber of commerce may have materials about writing a business plan geared to a small or part-time business. Books and computer programs are available, but they're probably beyond the scope of what you need unless you're going into a full-time

Hobbyists—Different Considerations

Starting a hobby-business means different planning considerations than starting a woodworking operation as a full-time job or sole means of support. You don't have to worry about having enough money saved to pay the mortgage while you get started. But you do need to consider how doing woodworking for money will affect your life. Will it take time away from work or family or other activities that you don't want to sacrifice? How will you limit the time you spend so that that demand doesn't overwhelm your ability to work at your own pace? And though you won't have to sell work to eat, you still need some kind of sales plan. The best work in the world won't sell if no one knows about it. And it won't sell very well if it's presented poorly, or in the wrong place.

business. If other resources fail, the Service Corps of Retired Executives (SCORE) may be able to help. SCORE, a branch of the Small Business Administration, can provide advice from a retired executive on virtually any business topic. Again, your local chamber of commerce or office of the SBA can put you in touch. And you can't beat talking to the people who know the most about what you're doing—woodworkers who have already started selling their work. Ask them about the problems they encountered and how they resolved them. Chances are, they'll be willing to share any wisdom they've acquired.

Handling Bigger Sales

One advantage of selling your work at craft shows and other direct-to-consumer outlets is that there's no credit risk. Your sales usually will be cash. You can spurn checks if you want. And you probably won't be taking credit cards. Larger sales—such as orders by retail stores or big-ticket commissioned pieces—can mean bigger problems. You can get stuck with lots of work for a deal that falls apart before you're paid. Or worse, you can be out the merchandise and the money.

Protecting yourself means getting things in writing. This doesn't have to be overly complicated. An extremely detailed document makes sales more time-consuming and thus harder to get. But you can provide yourself most of the protection you'll need with a simple sales agreement, purchase order or estimate sheet that includes:

- Description, quantity and price of the order
- Date of transaction
- Names, addresses and phone numbers of all parties
- Delivery date
- Payment terms
- Name and address of the customer
- Terms allowing additional charges for alterations in work or order not originally specified
- Dated signatures of you and the customer
- Releases that get you off the hook in case of unforeseeable events like natural disasters and work stoppages by suppliers

Should there be a problem or misunderstanding, this form can give you some documentation to support your position. Once you finish the job or fill the order, you can use the form as a bill or attach it as a copy to an invoice.

In the real world, woodworkers don't always have documentation for every sale. This is no problem when you know and trust the customer. Ultimately, that's far better security than a piece of paper ever provides.

Payment terms vary depending on such factors as type of work you do, the size of the project, etc. If

Planning Helps Executive Carve Second Career

Clark Pearson decided he didn't want to get pushed around the country anymore. Thanks to plans he had made to turn his wood carving hobby into a new career, he didn't have to be.

As vice president and general manager for the giant appliance maker White Consolidated Industries, he had been transferred from New Jersey to Pennsylvania to Ohio. But Pearson, then 52, said no thanks when White told him he was being transferred to Richmond, Indiana. Two years before, Pearson anticipated the transfer. Instead of resigning himself to another move, he developed a plan.

The Pearsons had decided they were "going to start enjoying our somedays," he says. Someday, they wanted

For Clark Pearson, turning his antique-reproduction wood carvings into a business in his rural Ohio home was part of "enjoying his somedays." But his success took plenty of planning. Even though Pearson started the venture three years ahead of schedule, his planning got him off to a fast start.

to run a business making antique-reproduction wood carvings. In 1985, they figured that someday would be 1990. So they started planning. Pearson had rekindled his boyhood interest in wood carving in the early 1980s while in Pennsylvania. He started selling his carvings at church bazaars. "That got me hooked on sitting there and people coming up and buying my things," he says. When he was transferred to Ohio, he started selling more of his carvings at craft shows.

But when he decided to do carvings as a career, Pearson knew he would need to do more than just attend craft shows. "My whole former business career had been in the marketing area," he says. "So I was quite familiar with the things a small company had to do."

First, the product line. Pearson made animals, birds and Christmas figures. He also made miniature toys and other figures based on postcards from the nineteenth century. His wife, Ronnie, developed a painting technique that makes each piece look antique.

Experience at craft shows had taught the Pearsons their pieces were popular. "But the craft shows became too much work," he says. "And when you do outdoor shows, you're at the mercy of the environment. So we decided to concentrate on the wholesale end of the business."

That meant they would need to do three things—start attending wholesale shows, develop professional-looking literature, and get some publicity that would make store owners and other wholesale buyers take notice.

"We needed good, descriptive literature with professionally done photography," he says. "In the hands of another business, that literature is your image. They don't know you. All they know is that literature." The Pearsons spent about $5,000 on photography, layout, copywriting, production and printing of a catalog. They had 10,000 printed, enough to last the five years they expected to be building a customer base before starting out full-time.

Ronnie Pearson is an essential part of "Delights of the Past." She paints each carving to give it an antique look. And she keeps the books and handles the correspondence.

But the catalog only works if someone requests it. So, Pearson set out to start building a name for himself with the stores, galleries and museum shops that would sell his folk art. He hired a publicist he had worked with previously in his job whose contacts with editors of such magazines as *Country Living, Early American Life, Colonial Homes, Country Homes* and *Country Decorating* helped lead to feature stories and national exposure with the consumers and retailers the Pearsons hoped to reach. Though they had to pay the publicist an hourly rate for her work, the exposure in the magazines came free of charge. The only problem was, they never knew when the stories would run. "It could be two or three months, or it could be two or three years," Clark says.

Fortunately, just as Clark gave notice to his old employer, *Colonial Homes* did a three-page spread on the Pearsons' work. "We got tremendous response. My wife would handle eighteen to twenty-five inquiries a day." They even had to hire a temporary employee. But it got their venture off to a fast start. Having the catalogs beforehand, he says, was crucial to making sales once the publicity got them noticed.

Getting into wholesale shows was the easiest part, Pearson says. They only had to submit slides of their work once to a show before their reputation allowed them to get in by just requesting a contract. They now do three wholesale shows a year, in Columbus, Ohio; Valley Forge, Pennsylvania; and Washington, D.C.

In all, the plan worked just right. The only glitch was that they had to go into business full-time three years before expected because the transfer came faster than anticipated. Thanks to the timing of publicity, however, they were ready faster, too.

Even with all the planning, the Pearsons still have slow times. Fortunately, they have enough money put aside to get through such times. Sometimes, they just take a working vacation. One year, the Pearsons traveled to Florida, visiting store owners they had only contacted by phone or mail in the past. Their visits generated enough orders that they had to cut their vacation short to start filling them.

you're doing work for a general contractor or interior designer, you can expect to bill when the work is done and be paid no later than thirty days after you bill. For sales to shops and galleries, terms vary widely—from consignment sales where payment isn't due until the item is sold, to COD or cash orders only. Ultimately, you'll decide what your terms are. If you're doing this as a hobby and don't depend on sales, there's little reason to take a credit risk on a new customer. Demanding cash up front will turn off some people. But that's not a problem if you don't need the sales badly. If you can't afford to miss sales because of credit terms, however, you may need to be flexible.

You should protect yourself as much as possible with new customers. That means:

- Getting cash before you deliver, or at least a deposit, if possible.
- If you do extend credit, do so only on a relatively small order. Insist on payment for an initial order before filling subsequent ones.
- Check credit ratings. Credit reports from Dun & Bradstreet usually aren't practical for a small business because of the price. But for a relatively small fee, you can join Support Services Alliance, a company that provides a number of services for small businesses, including credit reporting on individuals. You may not be able for run a credit check on the store, but you can run one on the proprietor, which should give you just as good an idea of creditworthiness.

If worse comes to worst and you get stiffed for a bill, you still have recourse. First, try gentle persuasion, reminding the customer by mail or phone that the bill is due, checking to make sure it wasn't lost, etc. If you've exhausted that outlet, and provided it's under the limit for a small claims suit in your state,

you can pursue the matter there fairly cheaply and easily. The limit is usually $1000 to $2500, depending on the state.

Small claims court can't help you if the customer is out of state or the claim is over the limit. In that case, you'd need to hire a lawyer, which could cost more than the bill did in the first place. If getting a small claims judgment doesn't get you your money, you're probably out of luck.

Cash—Getting It and Handling It

Simply put, cash flow is what goes into your checking account compared to what's coming out.

There are three ways you can get into a cash flow bind. The normal ups and downs that any venture faces are one way. Bills don't stop coming just because income is slow. So, if you don't have a reserve to deal with slow times, you could be in trouble. You also may face cash flow troubles merely by putting off sending out bills. That slows down payments you receive, while bills you incurred doing a project stack up. Another likely cash flow problem is inventory. Stockpiles of materials or unsold products tie up your money in a way that doesn't pay you interest or allow you to get liquid cash in a hurry.

The solutions to these problems are fairly simple. Doing them is a little harder.

- *Try to gear your selling activity so that work comes in fairly steadily—or at least try to level the peaks and valleys. A lull in work is a good time to do some selling. But don't get on a roller coaster by binging on projects, then binging on sales efforts, which results in another rush of projects. Try to sell even when you're busy pro-*

ducing, and do some preparatory production work in advance of projects when things are slow. If cycles are unavoidable, make sure you put aside enough cash in good times to tide you through the bad. Ohio part-time toy-maker Larry Joseph (see pages 58-59) knows most of his sales will be during the Christmas shopping season. So, after fall craft shows, he puts aside as much as he can into certificates of deposit that mature during summer months. That keeps income steady. He and his family also do just enough shows during summer, which is their main production time, to restock their supply shelves.

- *Bill regularly.* Either send a bill with an order or when a job is done, or set aside a regular time each week or month to bill.

- *Keep inventory as low as possible.* Have enough supplies on hand to take care of no more than a month's production or less. Keep track of how much you use and order more based on that. A regular ordering schedule based on what's actually used can keep inventory from building up. Likewise, don't finish work on speculation. At least have some idea of where you're going to sell something before you make it, even if you don't have an order in hand yet.

CHAPTER •Checklist

ADDRESS TAX CONSIDERATIONS
- ☐ Does the IRS consider you a business or a hobby?
- ☐ Home-shop/office deductions
- ☐ Equipment deductions
- ☐ Skills improvement deductions

DEVELOPING A BUSINESS PLAN
- ☐ What is your specialty?
- ☐ Who will buy what you make?
- ☐ How do you get to your customers?
- ☐ What kind of promotion do you need?
- ☐ What are your costs?
- ☐ How do you compensate yourself?
- ☐ How much do you need to invest?
- ☐ Can you start small and then grow?
- ☐ How much money do you want to make?
- ☐ What legal requirements must you meet?

PROTECT YOURSELF AND YOUR SALES
- ☐ Use detailed sales agreements, purchase orders or estimate sheets
- ☐ Get cash, or at least a deposit, before you deliver
- ☐ Extend credit only on relatively small orders
- ☐ Insist on payment on initial orders before filling subsequent ones
- ☐ Check credit ratings

WORK ON GETTING AND HANDLING CASH
- ☐ Gear your selling activity to keep work steady
- ☐ Bill regularly
- ☐ Keep inventory as low as possible

CHAPTER NINE

Honing Your Skills

U p to now, this book has dealt with how to make money with your woodworking. This chapter looks at some of the opportunities that can make your woodworking more enjoyable and even more profitable.

Modern woodworkers have access to more opportunities to improve their craft than any woodworkers in history. Almost all of these opportunities, however, cost money. That's one place where profits from selling your work come in handy. The more money you make, the more you can spend improving your skills. The more you improve your skills, the more money you can make.

Among the learning opportunities:

- *TV shows.* This is one option that's free, or virtually free. The growing popularity of woodworking has spawned several national and local public television and cable programs for woodworkers. Probably the most popular is *New Yankee Workshop* on PBS, which tackles a different cabinetmaking or carpentry project each week. Scott Phillips's public TV program, *The American Woodshop,* is a newer show that targets somewhat less experienced woodworkers. It spends more time than *New Yankee Workshop* showing all the steps in a project, and though the projects are simpler, they're usually very original. Phillips relies on a more realistic selection of tools for the average woodworker, featuring a mix of hand and power tools. And his show features weekly profiles of a top professional woodworker or some historic or technical facet of woodworking. With a VCR, you can build from these shows a video library of future projects, and plans are available from both shows for a fee.
- *Books.* The growing number of woodworker's supply stores in major cities around the country have a rapidly growing variety of project and skill-building books for every woodworking specialty and skill level. Traditional bookstores have a more limited offering. And public libraries, while a good source of "free" books, are also fairly limited in selection. If you don't live close to a store or library with a good selection of woodworking books, or if you prefer the convenience of ordering from home, woodworkers' catalogs and the WoodWorker's Book Club are good ways to get books by mail. It won't be hard to get on catalog mailing lists. Just subscribe to almost any woodworking publication and you'll soon have all you want—and probably more.
- *Videos.* A growing number of project and skill-building videos for woodworkers are also available through woodworkers' supply stores or catalogs. Libraries may also carry some, but a much smaller selection than stores. These videos may cost the same or slightly less than a book and cover a more limited area. But there's nothing like actually seeing the work step by step to get an idea of how to do it.
- *Magazines and publications.* Along with the explosion in woodworking books and videos has been an equally large expansion of woodworking magazines. These range from project-oriented publications to publications with a mix of news, profiles of woodworkers and shop hints. Magazines for very specific specialties, such as wood turners, carvers, wooden boat enthusiasts and others can give you even more detailed information. They don't need to be woodworking publications to make you a better woodworker. Magazines covering your specialty—antiques, Early American styles, birds, whatever—can also be valuable sources on trends and discoveries that inspire new work or help you serve customers better.

Courses: Getting Hands-on Experience From Pros

All the above routes will improve your work. But none is quite so enjoyable as a woodworking class. As with everything else in woodworking, the options here expand almost by the week. They range from local continuing-education classes and seminars to courses by nationally recognized artisans at special schools. Here's a closer look at your options.

- *Local continuing and vocational education.* Colleges, high schools and vocational schools frequently offer noncredit woodworking classes. Most are fairly basic, but you may be surprised. Depending on the level of interest in your town, more advanced classes may be offered as well. Contact the high schools and vocational schools near you to get on their mailing list for adult education classes. And check with local universities on their continuing education offerings.

- *Seminars and classes by woodworkers' supply stores, equipment dealers, etc.* Some of these are really more like equipment demos and thinly veiled pitches. But some are quite valuable short courses taught by talented local woodworkers. The only way to find out for sure is to attend. And since these shows are usually free or offered for a nominal charge, they're not a bad deal even if you don't learn much.

- *Seminars and classes by local experts.* These can be one of the best values. Skilled local artisans often supplement their income by teaching classes in their studios or in connection with local galleries, businesses or woodworking clubs.

PHOTO BY GLENDA TENNANT NEFF

Wood carving instructor Red Rainey demonstrates relief carving techniques to students at the John C. Campbell Folk School in Brasstown, North Carolina. The school is one of several around the country that give woodworkers the chance to learn new skills and enjoy a vacation in a beautiful setting.

Such classes cost more than some others. But with smaller class sizes and expert teaching, you get what you pay for. Inquire at a local woodworkers' supply store about any private classes that might be available in your area. There may be postings in the store, or employees may know where to steer you. Woodworking publications also frequently list courses being offered around the country in calendar or classified listings.

- *College-level programs.* Some colleges and universities around the country offer woodworking programs or classes for credit, or even major courses of study. These are more in-depth, and more costly than continuing education classes, but they can be a good supplement to your skills or even lead to a degree if you so desire.

- *National schools and seminars.* Several nationally recognized schools for artisans offer classes by top national artisans in a variety of woodworking specialties. The John C. Campbell Folk School in Brasstown, North Carolina; Kunkel Brothers School of Professional Woodworking in

Flanders, New Jersey; and the Arrowmont School in Gatlinburg, Tennessee, are a few examples. The Great Smoky Mountain Region of Tennessee and North Carolina probably has more good schools per square mile than any area of the U.S. Such schools can provide excellent learning vacations, since they're often set in or near tourist areas. See the Appendix for a listing of some of the major schools. They will be glad to send you detailed information about their programs.

Learning From Other Woodworkers

One of the cheapest and most enjoyable ways to expand your woodworking horizons is to learn from fellow woodworkers informally through local clubs. General woodworking clubs, and more specialized clubs for carvers, turners and others, abound across the country. Some are local chapters of national groups or strictly local organizations. Checking calendar listings in woodworking magazines or your local newspaper is one way to find them. You can also tap this network by asking around at craft shows or woodworkers' supply stores. If you can't find a group that works for you, start one of your own.

Joining a club can help you hone your skills in a variety of ways.

- Meetings are good ways for members to exchange tips informally.
- Clubs can arrange for top artisans to speak. Often local woodworkers will do this for free, but if you have to pay, it helps to share the fee with club members.
- Clubs usually are a mix of professionals and serious amateur woodworkers. Not only can you pick up technical and business advice, but you also may find bargains on used tools and equipment being sold by other members of the club. As more experienced woodworkers move up to better tools, their used tools may be just right for you.
- Clubs may also be able to arrange group discounts from stores, publishers and other suppliers.
- Besides pooling information, you may also be able to swap specialized work with other woodworkers to add extra touches to a project. That's one reason why a club that combines cabinetmakers, turners and carvers can be valuable.
- Clubs also can help hone your marketing efforts. You can swap information about local shows and stores. Or you can develop selling partnerships with woodworkers who make complementary products—such as a maker of antique-reproduction furniture with a maker of period-style accessory items.

Generally, even competitive woodworkers are willing to share information with each other because of their common bond. If you look at club membership as a chance to give and receive, you can expect success.

How Hobbyists Become Pros

With woodworking, the line between hobbyist and pro is ultra-fine, if in fact it really exists. The usual yardsticks just don't apply. There are people who make selling their woodworking a full-time job and still turn out fairly amateurish-looking stuff. Some "professional" woodworkers in huge mills are really more like factory workers who have no particular

Fantastic finish a great start for woodworking business

It's the last step, and one that even some experienced woodworkers often feel some trepidation in taking. Finishing a project can take as much experience and skill as putting it together in the first place. And because it takes special expertise, it also can be the makings of a great niche.

Susanne Noble sands a cabinet door before applying finish.

Partners Susanne Noble and Bill Lindenschmidt found that was the case when they formed Noble Finishing Co. in 1985 in Cincinnati. Noble was a finisher and Lindenschmidt a wood machinist for a large Cincinnati shop when they started their first independent moonlighting job restoring woodwork in executive offices for a marketing research company in the former Post Times-Star newspaper building.

The project led them to think about starting a business of their own, rather than working for someone else the rest of their lives. Noble took a night class on how to start a small business. After three years of working part time in the finishing business, she quit her day job to start Noble Finishing in 1988. A few months later, her work load had grown to the point that Lindenschmidt joined her in the business full time.

While many shops locally and nationally specialize in restoration, much of the work for Noble Finishing is in finishing new pieces. Noble Finishing's business actually breaks down into three main categories—finishing new pieces for small cabinet shops and interior designers, smaller restoration and refinishing jobs for businesses, and major refinishing projects for companies or real estate developers. This type of finishing work has provided fairly consistent growth for the four-employee company.

The finishing business has a sort of built-in stabilizing effect, Noble has found. When work on new pieces lags because of a poor economy, work on restoration and refinishing seems to go up, because more people and businesses refurbish old furniture or woodwork rather than buying new.

A finishing business doesn't have the big investment in wood and the wide array of tools most other woodworking businesses have. But it's still far from cheap to set up the right way. In retrofitting a new location with a properly ventilated spray booth, air-makeup system and loading dock, the company recently spent $35,000.

The expense of doing the job right is one reason even many professional shops turn to Noble Finishing. The other is their expertise, which has been proven through a variety of projects.

Since the first big job, Noble Finishing has done several other large, prominent restoration projects in Cincinnati. They restored zebrawood in Union Terminal, a once-mothballed train station that is seeing new life as a combination station and museum center. "They didn't have heat on or anythng in there for years," Lindenschmidt says. "Some of it was coming off the walls, and the rest was in really bad shape." Where the zebrawood had disappeared completely, they replaced it with veneer which was being removed from other areas of the station. In other cases, they drew in missing details. "With zebrawood, a lot of it was drawn in originally anyway," Lindenschmidt says.

In another major project, the finishers' sleight of hand was almost too good. The company put a marbleized finish on wood in the restored arcade of the Carew Tower, a 1929 skyscraper that's still Cincinnati's tallest building. "Our marbleizing was so good that some of the maintenance crew thought it was real marble," Lindenschmidt says. "They wanted to clean it off with lacquer thinner before we told them they shouldn't do that."

Big jobs can be a mixed blessing for a shop the size of Noble Finishing. "It can get tight in the middle of a big project," Noble says, "especially if the client is unwilling to give a deposit or do a partial billing." Fortunately, Noble also has a good mix of steady work from smaller restoration projects. For instance, the company gets a steady stream of business restoring the wood paneling in downtown elevators for Otis Elevator Co. Corporate clients also hire the company to touch up conference tables, office furniture or wood paneling in executive offices. Conference tables in particular can be big ticket jobs, Lindenschmidt says, with billings reaching thousands of dollars.

Another lucrative niche for Noble Finishing has been offering service contracts for corporate clients to maintain their furniture and paneling. "Wood is so expensive now that companies are realizing how much it costs," Lindenschmidt says. "They don't want to just let it deteriorate and replace it, because it's not cheap anymore." Noble offers companies service contracts, with prices based on the amount of wood they have. Under the contract, the company will inspect furniture, paneling and woodwork quarterly, semi-annually or annually and refinish as necessary.

Unlike many refinishers, Noble Finishing does few small "retail" jobs, such as touching up dining room tables, Noble says. Except for the occasional job for a friend, the shop works strictly with trade customers.

One of the company's first and best clients has been Globe Business Interiors, a Cincinnati office furniture supplier. When furniture is scratched or damaged during delivery, the company calls out Noble for on-the-spot troubleshooting, often overnight and sometimes out of town.

"It's saving them quite a bit of money over having to send the pieces back to the factory," Lindenschmidt says. "We usually can come in that very night and repair it by the next morning, so the client is happy."

Noble, who says the company has done little formal marketing, traces most of the company's business to referrals from Ray Spangler, a Globe sales representative. Supplier's sales representatives have also helped spread the word to small cabinet shops they call on in the area.

When home construction and consumer confidence are riding high, Noble Finishing gets most of its work from small cabinet shops that don't have their own spray booths or finishing expertise. "We can help small cabinetmakers to get into the high-end stuff that they otherwise wouldn't be equipped to handle," Noble says. Cabinet shops that specialize in laminate work but want wood doors for a particular project also may turn to Noble. In some cases, Noble says her shop can turn around a job in a few days when a supplier of ready-made components might need several weeks. For one job, a cabinet shop turned to Noble Finishing to apply a white lacquer finish with which it had no experience. "They realized they had no way of doing it themselves," she says. "So it opens up a whole new market for them this way."

Other work for new projects comes from interior designers, who call the company in to consult on finishes for some new pieces.

Noble Finishing doesn't claim a signature style for its work, but it is distinguished by quality, Lindenschmidt says. "We've lost money on a lot of jobs because, if it doesn't look right, we don't want it to go out. We've had clients accept a piece, but we're still not satisfied."

Noble is always willing to try something new. The company has worked with everything from gold leaf to automotive paint. For one recent project, a client wanted his condo's kitchen cabinets painted the same metallic black as his Jaguar. Noble used the genuine article, applying and buffing out 20 coats of Jaguar lacquer for a super-high-gloss finish.

"I've started doing more decorative finishes, even people's walls and ceilings," Noble says. "Still most of the decorative finishes are on furniture. That part of the business is really increasing. I'm doing a lot of gold leaf or 18th century or Oriental kinds of finishes on pieces."

interest in their craft. And there are hobbyists who do the work of skilled masters and have never sold a piece in their lives.

You can be a "pro" and still treat your woodworking as a hobby. The whole point is to enjoy it. Selling your work is one aspect of being a pro, but that alone won't make you one. Hobbyists become pros because they love woodworking. That drives people to keep improving skills, to keep learning the history, science and lore behind their special area of woodworking. What you learn in this book can be part of that process.

Craftsman turns old log and timber houses into new homes

As long as there are old log and timber-frame houses around, Terry Sawyer won't run out of raw materials. At least if he can keep the fire departments away.

The Kentucky craftsman specializes in building new homes out of old log and timber barns and houses. He disassembles the old, salvages what he can, and uses as little new material as possible in rebuilding historically accurate log and timber homes for his customers.

His reputation is such that he always has a waiting list of two or three customers. Though he hires two or three laborers each summer to help with the work, he still has trouble keeping up with demand.

Fire departments are a different problem. They get their practice burning down Sawyer's main source of materials. "I try to get there before they do," says Sawyer. Usually he succeeds. He has an inventory of five or so old

Terry Sawyer nails in the interior window frame of a two-story log house addition in Union, Kentucky (below).

structures that land owners have agreed to let him take away. And he stores about two barns worth of old wood in his home workshop. He hasn't faced any shortage of salvage prospects, or customers, yet.

Sawyer may be in the perfect place to ply his unusual trade. The Northern Kentucky suburbs of Cincinnati are growing rapidly. Subdivisions and commercial de-

velopments are springing up on old tobacco or horse farms. The real estate investors or developers who own the land see the old buildings on them more as nuisances than assets, so they usually let Sawyer take them away for free. It doesn't hurt, either, that Cincinnati was the most populous urban area west of the Alleghenies until after the Civil War, leaving a wealth of 19th-century wood structures in Southern Ohio and Northern Kentucky. When they come down, there's a good chance Terry Sawyer will be there to get them.

Terry Sawyer & Sons (mostly Terry, since his sons were both pre-teens when he started the business and won't be out of high school until 2002) builds one or two houses each year, along with an addition and a few remodeling projects. Sawyer says it's hard to predict his annual revenues. But with each major house project costing $100,000 or more, sales average $150,000 to $200,000 a year.

Sawyer does most jobs on a time-plus-material basis. But most of the material is free, and he charges only $15 an hour. Sawyer says he usually can build a 2500- to 3000-square-foot home for $110,000 to $130,000. Besides salvaging and re-erecting old timber buildings, Sawyer also does the blueprints, and often the plumbing, electrical work, finish work and much of the concrete work. "I work too cheaply," he admits. "But I have fun doing it."

Sawyer started salvaging and rebuilding vintage wood in 1979, after a friend, Lowell Scott, bought the tiny hamlet of Rabbit Hash, about 30 miles downstream of Cincinnati on the Ohio River. He helped Scott restore a general store, antique store and houses in Rabbit Hash. That led to referrals for other jobs in and around the hamlet. A book on timber framing and experience helped him learn the craft.

For one of his early projects, Sawyer helped another friend, photographer Randy Cochran, build a 3500-square-foot house in Rabbit Hash almost entirely from salvaged materials, working in phases over three years. They started by salvaging more about 80 22'-long hemlock timbers from a nearby building that was being demolished. Cochran, who lived in another house along the Ohio River during the building project, used a boat to gather cherry and walnut boards that would float downstream during floods or high waters. Those were later used for trim, doors and window frames.

But Sawyer usually has to do more than wait for wood to float down the river. He looks for signs of new development and asks the landowners if he can take away the old buildings. Sometimes he gets tips from a friend who is historic preservation officer for Boone County, Kentucky.

Sawyer finds he needs a house and half of salvaged wood for every new one he builds. "Unless there's water damage in the timbers, they're all usable," he says. Log houses yield about 75-percent usable wood, compared to only about 50 percent for barns. Most of the remaining scrap is just a result of having to recut the wood to fit the new plans.

Working with salvaged wood sometimes means having to improvise. Sawyer pointed out in one home he built a walnut post that joins a loft railing with the top of the stairway banister. The post rests about a foot short of the floor.

Sawyer's customers, however, don't seem to mind the idiosyncrasies of working with salvaged wood. Any problems are more than offset by the primitive look and the historical value.

"A 100-year-old floor is a lot prettier than any $3-a-foot hardwood floor you can go out and buy," he says. "You can't just make it look 100 years old. It's hard to get the colors in it. . . . There's a lot of beauty you just can't buy."

A desire for historical authenticity moved Dan Wilson, a Union, Kentucky, juvenile counselor and avid history buff who participates in Revolutionary War re-enactments, to ask Sawyer to help build an addition to his home. Though the home has aluminum siding put on by a former owner, the Wilsons have exposed the original logs on the inside. When Wilson wanted an addition, he chose Sawyer to help him preserve the historic integrity. Sawyer found a 27'×33' log cabin to provide materials for the 27'×30' addition.

"We're not trying to make a modern log home," Wilson says. "We're trying to make it look as historically correct as possible. We're not putting big picture or bay windows in. We're trying to use the old window systems and using mainly all solid or all natural materials." Sawyer and Wilson used round log rafters with the bark still on, much of the original hardware from the old cabin, and windows removed from another log house. Sawyer carved new mortises into the logs with an ax and adze, though he used a power table saw to cut window frames.

One other concession to modernity was using a 220-volt pressurized washer to clean the old logs. Not only did the power washing remove the old gray surface and return the brown color of the original logs: it also removed dirt and dust that could cause problems for Wilson's wife, who has asthma.

One drawback to salvaged wood is the need for periodic treatment with wood preservatives and insecticides to keep bugs off, particularly powder post beetles. But Wilson points out that termites aren't as much of a threat, since the sap that attracts them has been gone from these logs for decades.

To look at some of the sagging barns from which Sawyer has taken wood, it's hard to believe they could yield materials for a new home. Sawyer admits that young couples have trouble making the mental leap from a dilapidated barn to the house of their dreams when he starts planning a project with them. But he says the quality of materials is actually superior to most new homes. "When you're using hardwood timbers, it's a lot more substantial house than what you can go out and stick together with 2×4s. It might be coming out of a barn that's 100 years old. But if you put it together right, it will stand up another 100 years. I wouldn't say that about some of these houses they're building today."

Chicago pair scrolls way to successful business

Roy King and Scott Kochendorfer of Oak Lawn, Illinois, have been friends since first grade, and they've been in business together, it seems, almost as long.

Roy King (right) and lifelong friend Scott Kochendorfer built up a part-time hobby into a full-time scroll saw pattern business.

Unfortunately, not all the businesses were nearly as fulfilling as the friendship. Their auto repair shop didn't pan out. Worm farming, though it seemed like a can't-miss proposition, never got off the ground either. Sure, trash-eating worms could save the environment, and worms multiply like nobody's business. But they didn't survive a hard winter. Then came the Desert Storm T-shirts. The war went well. But the speed of the allied troops caught King and Kochendorfer almost as much off guard as the Iraqis. By the time they agreed on the perfect design and got the shirts printed, the war was almost over and the market was evaporating.

Only by accident did the two Chicago-area men stumble on their most successful venture. King took up scroll-saw crafts as a hobby, not really thinking about a new business at the time. He bought a $50 Dremel scroll saw, the kind with suction cups that attach to a wall. And in seemingly no time at all he had gone through just about every pattern he could find in books. "I had more than 200 cut-out animals," King says, "and I got kind of bored with it."

So he bought himself an $800 Delta scroll saw, thinking a better tool could help him get more out of his hobby. "But I was asking myself, what are you going to do with it? And my wife asked me the same thing. That made me think a little harder and look at patterns a little harder."

That led him to start adding a few frills of his own by cutting additional lines into some patterns. Then, by chance, he was playing with one of his cut-outs one day and dropped it on top of another piece. "And I thought, hey, this looks pretty good! I put some spacing behind it, and that's when this all started."

The crux of the idea was 3-D scroll-saw patterns, which added a whole new dimension to the hobby. King didn't recognize it as a commercial venture at first. he just made about a dozen scroll-saw plaques for himself and his family. Then friends started noticing them and asking him to make some for them. Before long, he put a few out at a church craft fair and ended up taking orders for $400 worth of plaques. Soon one customer, a nun, placed an order for 50 plaques at $50 each, which netted a $500 to $600 profit.

The popularity of the 3-D pieces made King think there was more to the business than craft fairs. With his old buddy Kochendorfer, he came up with the idea of selling 3-D scroll saw patterns and developed a catalog.

At first, the new business took off slowly. They took out an ad in *Popular*

Mechanics, which, while inexpensive, only generated about 40 or 50 orders. Then, they decided to go the publicity route. Never ones to think small, they started with the largest-circulation woodworking magazine, *Better Homes & Gardens Wood*. Like many other guys with ideas and products, they called editor Larry Johnson. He invited them to send a sample of their work, which they did, via next-day mail. Johnson saw enough in it to do a small feature on their patterns. And that generated enough response for the magazine to do a feature article. "It really took off after that," Kochendorfer says. "Before that, we were doing it part-time. Then once they did a feature on us (in February 1993) we had to quit our jobs."

Of course, that was the idea all along. Kochendorfer had been service manager for 15 years for a local Ford dealership. King had been a city truck dispatcher for a local company. "It was kind of cut and dried," King says. "Just pounding out the old jobs."

The secret for the success of their new company, Scroller Ltd., is that the two really love it. Kochendorfer was no woodworker before he started, he admits. It took him about seven tries at his first eagle pattern to create something he considered presentable. But now, he loves it as much as King. And it shows. About 700 patterns later, King and Kochendorfer, along with their wives and part-time seasonal employ-ees they hire, still answer the phones and take orders. And they take the time to talk with customers on the phone about patterns, scroll-sawing or whatever.

"At times we spend an hour or two with customers on the phone," Kochendorfer says. "In a couple of cases, we probably taught people to scroll saw over the phone. But we never get tired of the questions. If they have a better finished product, then they're going to come back to us and buy more. You've got to love it, and it's got to be genuine. There's no phony baloney here. We get excited about it when we talk to people. It's not made up. I'm not sure you can make it up after three years."

Knowing customers is also key to making the business grow, Kochendorfer says. That knowledge comes in part from talking to customers. For instance, they've learned to provide a wide range of difficulty levels, which are rated in the Scroller category from 1 to 10. Novices need to be convinced that the patterns are easier than they look, despite the many fine lines. Experts need to be fed a constant stream of new challenges. No pattern every goes into the catalog until King and Kochendorfer have tested and tweaked it themselves.

Besides the hands-on, however, the business relies on using a computer and database software to understand their customers through statistics. "You can be searching and struggling and it's impossible to get to the next level until you know who your customers are and what they want to see," Kochendorfer says. "And the only way to track that is with a computer."

Engineer follows rising tide of interest in wooden boats

Jack McCarthy left a high-paying job as a mechanical engineer in 1979 to do something he loved—restoring wood boats. What he loved also turned out to be a profitable venture. McCarthy launched his business into a rising tide of nostalgic interest in classic wooden boats in the Cincinnati area and nationwide.

Today, McCarthy's Wooden Boat Shop in Cincinnati's Sayler Park neighborhood near the Ohio River is one of the best regarded wooden boat restoration shops in the country. Besides the growth of collector interest in antique wooden boats, McCarthy credits his efforts to treat clients fairly and guide their interest in the hobby as elements of his success.

"It used to be a strange sight seeing a wooden boat on the Ohio River," he says. "Now it's becoming almost a daily sight."

He describes typical wooden boat enthusiasts as "rich and powerful" people who've reached middle age and are trying to recapture some of their lost youth. But trying to take advantage of collectors' wealth won't work, McCarthy believes. He prefers to cultivate customers with reasonable prices for quality work. That's because word-of-mouth reputation is everything in the still fairly small, close-knit world of antique boat collecting. Some restoration shops haven't been able to resist the urge to overcharge for their work, he says. And as a result, their customer base disappeared.

As an active member of the Cincinnati Antique Boat club and organizer of Cincinnati boat shows, McCarthy also does what he can to build interest in wooden boats. And he likes to coach potential customers on boat purchases. "I accept all the calls," he says. "They're all potential customers."

Some collectors may do part of the restoration themselves. "There's one doctor who will varnish the boat himself until he gets it down to two more coats," McCarthy says. "Then he'll bring it to us to finish it."

Most jobs are more complicated and painstaking than that. Many antique boats have been left outside, neglected to the ravages of the elements for years. McCarthy often has to replace substantial portions of the mahogany hulls to restore such boats. Planks are always hand-shaped, and most of the sanding must be done by hand, just as it would be done on fine mahogany furniture.

As with most hobbies, wooden boat collecting has its purists. Some seek the original hardware, even the original wiring, when restoring boats. So, as a sideline, McCarthy runs a mail-order business in original and reproduction wooden parts, hardware and spar varnish. "If we're going to do a comprehensive job," he says, "we have to have all of this stuff."

McCarthy wouldn't have gotten into wooden boat restoration if he hadn't been an avid hobbyist himself. Fortunately, he also had a solid footing in woodworking. His father, John F. McCarthy, spent his career making wood floors in Cincinnati. And the younger McCarthy restored boats part-time to work his way through the University of Cincinnati for his engineering degree.

But after ten years as an engineer, he realized he was fed up with the business world. "You get to the point where you've had enough of the corporate politics," he says. "I'm doing what I always wanted to do and making a living at it. It's not quite the $50,000 to $60,000 a year I used to make. Then again, I don't have high blood pressure. And I don't even have to set an alarm, because I look forward to coming to work."

CHECK OUT LEARNING OPPORTUNITIES

☐ TV shows

☐ Books

☐ Videos

☐ Magazines and publications

☐ Courses

　　—Local continuing education and vocational classes

　　—Seminars and classes by dealers and manufacturers

　　—Seminars and classes by local experts

　　—College-level programs

　　—National schools and seminars

☐ Other woodworkers, clubs and associations

Appendix

Books

The Encyclopedia of Wood
Sterling Publishing Co. Inc., 1989
387 Park Ave. S.
New York, NY 10016

WoodWorker's Book Club
P.O. Box 12171
Cincinnati, OH 45212-0171

The Woodworker's Guide to Pricing Your Work
Dan Ramsey, 1994
Betterway Books
1507 Dana Ave.
Cincinnati, OH 45207

*The Woodworker's Guide to
Selecting and Milling Wood*
Charles Self, 1994
Betterway Books
1507 Dana Ave.
Cincinnati, OH 45207

Woodworker's Handbook
Roger W. Cliffe, 1990
Sterling Publishing Co. Inc.
387 Park Ave. S.
New York, NY 10016

Woodworker's Source Book (2nd Edition)
Charles Self, 1995
Betterway Books
1507 Dana Ave.
Cincinnati, OH 45207

Working at Woodworking
Jim Tolpin, 1990
The Taunton Press Inc.
Newtown, CT 06740-5506

Organizations

American Association of Woodturners
667 Harriet Ave.
Shoreview, MN 55126

American Craft Association
21 S. Elkins Corner Road
Highland, NY 12528

American Craft Retailers Association
P.O. Box 9
Woodstock, MD 21163

Forest Products Laboratory
1 Gifford Pinchot Dr.
Madison, WI 53705

IRS Tax Information and Pamphlets
800/424-1040

National Wood Carvers Association
7424 Miami Ave.
Cincinnati, OH 45243
(One of the best values of any kind in America. For
$11, you get a membership card and subscription to
semimonthly full-color glossy magazine *Chip Chats.*)

Service Corps of Retired Executives
National Headquarters
409 3rd St. NW
Washington, DC 20416

Support Services Alliance Inc.
P.O. Box 130
Schoharie, NY 12157

Volunteer Lawyers for the Arts
1 East 53rd St.
Sixth Floor
New York, NY 10022
(Can make referrals to local chapters around the
country, some of which also offer accounting services or referrals to accountants.)

Woodworking Association of North America
Main St.
Falmouth, MA 02540

Publications

American Woodworker
400 S. 10th St., Dept. 81000
Emmaus, PA 18098

Art & Antiques
Trans World Publishing Co.
633 Third Ave.
New York, NY 10017

Better Homes and Gardens Wood
1912 Grand Ave.
Des Moines, IA 50309-3379

Colonial Homes
Hearst Corp.
1700 Broadway, 28th Floor
New York, NY 10019

Country Home
Meredith Corp.
750 3rd Ave.
New York, NY 10017

Country Living
Hearst Corp.
5400 S. 60th St., Box 643
Greendale, WI 53129

The Crafts Report
The Crafts Report Publishing Co.
700 Orange St.
Wilmington, DE 19801
(Indispensable for anyone selling crafts.)

Early American Life
Cowles Magazines Inc.
Box 8200
Harrisburg, PA 17105

Fine Woodworking
The Taunton Press
63 S. Main St., Box 5506
Newtown, CT 06470-5506

Modern Woodworking
Target Magazine Group
167 E. Hwy. 72
Collierville, TN 38017

Popular Woodworking
1507 Dana Ave.
Cincinnati, OH 45207

Sunshine Artists
Palm House Publishing
2600 Temple Dr.
Winter Park, FL 32789
(This is a good source for reviews and ratings of craft
shows around the country.)

WoodenBoat
Naskeag Rd.
Brooklin, ME 04616

Woodshop News
35 Pratt St.
Essex, CT 06426
(A must for any woodworker selling work.)

Woodwork
Ross Periodicals
P.O. Box 1529
Ross, CA 94957
(Profile-oriented publication can give you good ideas
from others who started selling their work.)

Woodworker's Business News
5604 Alameda Place NE
Albuquerque, NM 87313

Workbench
KC Publishing
700 W. 47th St., Suite 310
Kansas City, MO 64112

Computer Software

Plywood Planner & Casp'er
10 Pike St.
Herminie, PA 15637

Schools and Seminars

Alpine School of Woodcarving Ltd.
225 Vine Ave.
Park Ridge, IL 60068

Anderson Ranch Arts Center
P.O. Box 5598
Snowmass Village, CO 81615

Arrowmont School of Arts and Crafts
P.O. Box 567
Gatlinburg, TN 37738

The Artizans College
P.O. Box 539
Sea St.
Rockport, ME 04856

Augusta Heritage Center
Davis and Elkins College
Elkins, WV 26241-3996

Brookfield Craft Center
P.O. Box 122
Brookfield, CT 06804

John C. Campbell Folk School
Rt. 1, Box 14A
Brasstown, NC 28902

Canterbury Shaker Village
288 Shaker Rd.
Canterbury, NH 03224

College of the Redwoods
Fine Woodworking Program
440 Alger St.
Fort Bragg, CA 95437

Conover Workshops
18125 Madison Rd.
Parkman, OH 44080

Cook Forest Sawmill Center for the Arts
P.O. Box 180
Cooksburg, PA 16217

Craft Students League
YWCA of New York City
610 Lexington Ave.
New York, NY 10022

Haystack Mountain School of Crafts
P.O. Box 518
Deer Isle, ME 04627

Drew Langsner
Country Workshops
90 Mill Creek Rd.
Marshall, NC 28753

Northwest School of Wooden Boatbuilding
251 Otto St.
Port Townsend, WA 98368

Peters Valley Craft Center
19 Kuhn Rd.
Layton, NJ 07851

Rhode Island School of Design
Office of Admissions
2 College St.
Providence, RI 02903

Rochester Institute of Technology
Office of Admissions
1 Lomb Memorial Dr.
P.O. Box 9887
Rochester, NY 14623-0887

Thousand Islands Craft School and Textile Museum
314 John St.
Clayton, NY 13624

Wood Carving School
3056 Excelsior Blvd.
Minneapolis, MN 55416

WoodenBoat School
P.O. Box 78
Brooklin, ME 04616

Wood Turning Center
P.O. Box 25706
Philadelphia, PA 19144

Yestermorrow
P.O. Box 344-1
Warren, VT 05674

Tools and Supplies

American Clockmaker
P.O. Box 326
Clintonville, WI 54929

American Woodcrafters Supply
212 E. Main Box G
Riceville, IA 50466

Apollo Sprayers International Inc.
1030 Joshua Way
Vista, CA 92083
(Spraying equipment)

Atlas Dowel & Wood Products Co.
5819 Filview Circle
Cincinnati, OH 45248

Bainbridge Manufacturing Inc.
7873 N.E. Day Rd.
Bainbridge Isle, WA 98110
(General hardware.)

Robert Bosch Power Tool Corp.
New Ridge Rd.
Hanover, MD 21076
(Router bits)

Brand Mark by F & K Concepts
462 Carthage Dr.
Beavercreek, OH 45434
(Branding irons/woodburning)

Buckeye Saw Company
4930 Provident Dr.
Cincinnati, OH 45246
(Router bits)

C.B. Tool & Supply Inc.
Karina Ct.
San Jose, CA 95131

Craft Supplies USA
Publisher of the Woodturner's Catalog
1287 East, 1120 South
Provo, UT 84601
(Supplier of high-quality wood lathes and wood turner's tools designed by Rude Osolnik and others.)

Craftsman Wood Service
1735 W. Courtland Ct.
Addison, IL 60101

Dremel
4915 21st St.
Racine, WI 53406

The Duck Blind
8721-B Gull Rd.
Richland, MI 49083
(Woodcarving tools/supplies)

Floral Glass & Mirror, Inc.
895 Motor Parkway
Hauppauge, NY 11788

Frank Mittermeier, Inc.
P.O. Box 2W
3577 E. Tremont Ave.
Bronx, NY 10465
(Woodcarving tools/supplies)

Garrett Wade Co.
161 Avenue of the Americas
New York, NY 10013

The Irwin Company
92 Grant St.
Wilmington, OH 45177

Joe Katona
J.K. Woodcraft
3398 Aquinas St.
Rochester, MI 48309

Keller & Co.
1327 "I" St.
Petaluma, CA 94952

Kuempel Chime Clockworks and Studio
21195 Minnetonka Blvd.
Excelsior, MN 55391

Lee Valley Tools, Ltd.
1080 Morrison Dr.
Ottawa, Ontario, Canada K2H 8K7

Leichtung Fine Tool Store
Mayfield Rd.
Cleveland, OH 44124

Leigh Industries Ltd.
P.O. Box 357
Port Coquitlam, British Columbia
Canada V3C 4K6

MLCS Ltd.
P.O. Box 4053
Rydal, PA 19046
(Maker of biscuit router bits.)

Paxton Hardware Ltd.
7818 Bradshaw Rd.
Upper Falls, MD 21156

Penn State Industries
2850 Comly Rd.
Philadelphia, PA 19154

Phantom Engineering
1122 S. State St., No. 21
Provo, UT 84606

Racal Health & Safety Inc.
7305 Executive Way
Frederick, MD 21701

Read Tool Design & Manufacturing Co. Inc.
Route 2, Box 207
Monticello, FL 32344

Red Hill Corp. Supergrit
P.O. Box 4234
Gettysburg, PA 17325
(Abrasives/sanding)

Renovator's Supply
7152 Renovator's Old Mill
Millers Falls, MA 01349
(Lighting fixtures/furniture hardware)

Ritter Mfg.
521 Wilber Ave.
Antioch, CA 94509
(Clamps, vises, workbenches)

The Sanding Catalogue
P.O. Box 3737
Hickory, NC 28603

Tools On Sale/Seven Corners Ace Hardware
216 West 7th St.
St. Paul, MN 55102

Wilke Machinery Co.
3230 Susquehanna Trail
York, PA 17402
(Clamps, vises, workbenches)

Wood Carvers Supply
P.O. Box 8928-C
Norfolk, VA 23503

Woodcrafters Tool & Supplies
212 NE 6th Ave.
Portland, OR 97232

Woodsmith Shop
2200 Grand Ave.
Des Moines, IA 50312

Woodworker's Supply Inc.
1108 N. Glenn Rd.
Casper, WY 82601

Hand Tools

The Old Tool Shop
(a.k.a. John Walter, The Tool Merchant)
208 Front St.
Marietta, OH 45750
(John Walter is one of the best sources in the country for old hand tools, including a full line of older and antique Stanley Tools, for collectors or woodworkers.)

St. James Bay Tool Co.
122 E. Main St.
Mesa, AZ 85201
(Sells antique tools and new tools with designs based on antique tools.)

Portable Power Tools

AEG Power Tool Corp.
P.O. Box 6003
New London, CT 06320

Black & Decker—Elu Woodworking Tools
10 North Park Dr.
Hunt Valley, MD 21030

Eagle American Corp.
124 Parker Ct., P.O.
Box 1099
Chardon, OH 44024

Hitachi Power Tools, USA
Steve Reynolds Blvd.
Norcross, GA 30093

Makita U.S.A., Inc.
14930 Northam Street
La Mirada, CA 90638

Porter-Cable Corp.
4825 Highway 45 North
Jackson, TN 38305

Trimtramp Ltd.
151 Carlingview Dr.,
Unit 11
Toronto, Ontario
Canada M9W 5S4

Stationary Power Tools

Blume Supply, Inc.
3316 South Blvd.
Charlotte, NC 28209

C.B. Tool & Supply Inc.
Karina Ct.
San Jose, CA 95131

Delta Int. Machine Corp.
246 Alpha Dr.
Pittsburgh, PA 15238

Lobo Power Tools
E. Slavson Ave.
Pico Rivera, CA 90660

Powermatic
Morrison Rd.
McMinnville, TN 37110

Hardwood Lumber/Veneers

Bristol Valley Hardwoods
4300 Route 64
Canandaigua, NY 14424

Catskill Mountain Lumber Co.
Benton Hollow Rd.
Woodborne, NY 12788

Certainly Wood/Hardwood Veneer Co.
11753 Big Tree Rd.
E. Aurora, NY 14052

Craftsman Wood Service
1735 W. Courtland Ct.
Addison, IL 60101

Cut and Dried Quality Hardwood
143 S. Cedros Ave.
Solana Beach, CA 92075

Eisenbrand Inc., Exotic Hardwoods
4100 Spencer St.
Torrance, CA 90503

Heartwood Owner-Builder School
Johnson Rd.
Becket, MA 01233

Johnson's Workbench
563 N. Cochran
Charlotte, MI 48813

St. Louis Hardwoods
3560 Chouteau Ave.
St. Louis, MO 63103

Steve H. Wall Lumber Co.
Rt. 1 Box 287
Mayodan, NC 27027

Willard Brothers Woodcutters
300 Basin Rd.
Trenton, NJ 08619

Woodcrafters Tool & Supplies
212 NE 6th Ave.
Portland, OR 97232

Adhesives/Glues

Borden, Inc.
180 E. Broad St.
Columbus, OH 43215

DAP, Inc.
Janney Rd.
Dayton, OH 45404

Franklin International
2020 Bruck St.
Columbus, OH 43207

Master Bond Inc.
154 Hobart St.
Hackensack, NJ 07601

Swift Adhesives
3100 Woodcreek Dr.
Downers Grove, IL 60515

Finishing Supplies

Color Caulk, Inc.
1696 W. Mill St. #14
Colton, CA 92324

Daly's Wood Products
Regal Rd. RR 7
Guelph, OR

Minwax Co., Inc.
15 Mercedes Dr.
Montvale, NJ 07645

Sharpening Services

Buckeye Saw Company
4930 Provident Dr.
Cincinnati, OH 45246

Tools Etc.
1567 S. Harbor Blvd.
Fullerton, CA 92632

Wilke Machinery Co.
3230 Susquehanna Trail
York, PA 17402

Index

More Great Books for Your Woodshop!

Desks You Can Customize—Customize your furniture to fit your personal style. With Graves's instruction and detailed drawings, you'll create a unique, individualized desk as you experiment with legs, doors, drawers, organizers and much more. *#70309/$19.99/128 pages/133 b&w illus./paperback*

Good Wood Routers—Get the most from your router with this comprehensive guide to hand-held power routers and table routing. You'll discover a world of information about types of routers, their uses, maintenance, set-up, precision table routing and much, much more. *#70319/$19.99/128 pages/550 color illus.*

Tune Up Your Tools—Bring your tools back to perfect working order and experience safe, accurate cutting, drilling and sanding. With this handy reference you'll discover how to tune up popular woodworking machines, instructions for aligning your tools, troubleshooting charts and many other tips. *#70308/ $22.99/144 pages/150 b&w illus./paperback*

Display Cabinets You Can Customize—Go beyond building to designing furniture. You'll receive step-by-step instructions to the base projects—the starting points for a wide variety of pieces, such as display cabinets, tables and cases. Then you'll learn about customizing techniques. You'll see how to adapt a glass front cabinet, put a profile on a cabinet by using molding, get a different look by using stained glass, changing the legs and much more! *#70282/$18.99/128 pages/150 b&w illus./paperback*

Tables You Can Customize—Learn how to build four types of basic tables—from a Shaker coffee table to a Stickley library table—then discover how to apply a wide range of variations to customize the pieces to fit your personal needs. *#70299/$19.99/128 pages/ 150 b&w illus./paperback*

Marvelous Wooden Boxes You Can Make—Master woodworker Jeff Greef offers plans for 20 beautiful, functional boxes, complete with drawings, cutting lists, numbered step-by-step instructions and color photographs. *#70287/$24.99/144 pages/67 color, 225 b&w illus.*

Good Wood Joints—Learn which joints are best for specific situations and how to skillfully make them. You'll discover joints for every application, the basics of joint cutting and much more! Plus, you'll find an ingenious chart that makes choosing the right joint for the job easy. All well-illustrated with step-by-step instructions for making joinery by machine or hand. *#70313/$19.99/128 pages/550 color illus.*

Getting the Very Best from Your Scroll Saw—You'll turn to this technique, pattern and project book to learn how to get professional-quality results every time. You'll get directions on it all from cutting dovetails to cutting metal to creating inlays, marquetry and intarsia mosaics. You'll discover how to make puzzles, gifts, games, toys, Victorian fretwork shelves, moldings and much more! *#70289/ $19.99/160 pages/200 b&w illus./paperback*

Make Your Own Jigs & Woodshop Furniture—Innovative jigs and fixtures will help you specialize your ordinary power tools without spending big money. You'll get plans for over 40 jigs and fixtures, 23 projects for a well-outfitted workshop and more! *#70249/ $24.99/144 pages/100 b&w, 100 color illus.*

Making Wooden Mechanical Models—Discover plans for 15 handsome and incredibly clever machines with visible wheels, cranks, pistons and other moving parts made of wood. Expertly photographed and complete with materials lists and diagrams, the plans call for a challenging variety of techniques and procedures. *#70288/$21.99/144 pages/341 illus./ paperback*

Woodworker's Guide to Selecting and Milling Wood—Save money on lumber as you preserve the great tradition of felling, milling and drying your own wood. Loads of full-color illustrations will help you identify the right wood for every job. *#70248/$22.99/144 pages/128 b&w illus., 32 color photos.*

Build Your Own Mobile Power Tool Centers—Learn how to "expand" shop space by building mobile workstations that maximize utility, versatility and accessibility of woodshop tools and accessories. *#70283/$19.99/ 144 pages/250 b&w illus./paperback*

Creating Your Own Woodshop—Discover dozens of economical ways to fill unused space with the woodshop of your dreams. Self shows you how to convert space, lay out the ideal woodshop, or improve your existing shop. *#70229/$18.99/128 pages/162 b&w photos/illus./paperback*

Building Fine Furniture from Solid Wood—You'll build beautiful wood furniture with 11 of Sadler's most popular projects complete with instructions, exploded drawings and detailed photographs. *#70230/ $24.95/160 pages/175 b&w, 35 color illus.*

How To Sharpen Every Blade in Your Woodshop—You know that tools perform best when razor sharp—yet you avoid the dreaded chore. This ingenious guide brings you plans for jigs and devices that make sharpening any blade short and simple! Includes jigs for sharpening boring tools, router bits and more! *#70250/$17.99/144 pages/157 b&w illus./paperback*

The Woodworker's Sourcebook, 2nd Edition—Shop for woodworking supplies from home! Self has compiled listings for everything from books and videos to plans and associations. Each listing has an address and telephone number and is rated in terms of quality and price. *#70281/$19.99/160 pages/50 illus.*

Basic Woodturning Techniques—Detailed explanations of fundamental techniques like faceplate and spindle turning will have you turning beautiful pieces in no time. *#70211/ $14.95/112 pages/119 b&w illus./paperback*

Woodworker's Guide to Pricing Your Work—Turn your hobby into profit! You'll find out how other woodworkers set their prices and sell their products. You'll learn how to estimate average materials cost per project, increase your income without sacrificing quality or enjoyment, build repeat and referral business, manage a budget and much more! *#70268/$18.99/160 pages/paperback*

Measure Twice, Cut Once—Achieve good proportion, clean cuts and snug fits every time! You'll learn what each measuring tool does, how to use it properly—even how to make your own. *#70210/$18.99/128 pages/ 143 illus./paperback*

The Stanley Book of Woodworking Tools, Techniques and Projects—Become a better woodworker by mastering the fundamentals of choosing the right wood, cutting tight fitting joints, properly using a marking gauge and much more. *#70264/$19.95/160 pages/ 400 color illus./paperback*